A is for Adventure...

And B is for Beaches,
C is for Caves,
D is for Drama,
E is for Eggs.

F is for Fossils,
G is for Glass Blowing,
H is for Hobby Shows...and so on, and so on.

Raising Kids on Purpose for the Fun of It has literally hundreds of fun ideas from A to Z that you and your family will love. But this is only a starting point. Feel free to invent your own! As author Gwen Weising says: "Dream your own adventures—and dream them big."

Enjoy!

Raising Kids on Purpose

for the Fun of it

Gwen Weising

Fleming H. Revell Company
Old Tappan, New Jersey

Scripture identified NAS is from the New American Standard Bible, © The Lockman Foundation 1960, 1962, 1963, 1968, 1971, 1972, 1973, 1975, 1977.
Scripture marked NIV is from the Holy Bible, New International Version. Copyright © 1973, 1978, 1984 International Bible Society. Used by permission of Zondervan Bible Publishers.
Scripture identified RSV is from the Revised Standard Version of the Bible, Copyrighted © 1946, 1952, 1971, by the Division of Christian Education of the National Council of the Churches of Christ in the United States of America, and is used by permission. All rights reserved.

Library of Congress Cataloging-in-Publication Data

Weising, Gwen.
    Raising kids on purpose for the fun of it / Gwen Weising.
      p.   cm.
    ISBN 0-8007-5322-4
    1. Parenting—United States. 2. Parenting—Moral and ethical aspects. 3. Family recreation—United States. 4. Family—Religious life. 5. Values—Study and teaching—United States. 6. Child rearing—Religious aspects—Christianity. I. Title.
HQ755.8.W425 1989
649'.1—dc 20   89-8469
                                                          CIP

Copyright © 1989 by Gwen Weising
Published by the Fleming H. Revell Company
Old Tappan, New Jersey 07675
Printed in the United States of America

Contents

TO those who shared the adventure with me
—Ed, Wendy, and Mark

And to all those who believed in this project

Introduction

The doctor came through the door and smiled. "Well, you can go home today," he said. "I know you're eager to get that new baby home."

Eager to get the new baby home? No, I wasn't eager to get the new baby home. I was *terrified*. I didn't want to go home yet. I wanted to stay at least until tomorrow. Then maybe I'd be more ready to go.

"If you check out by noon, you won't have to pay for another day." He was still smiling. I was terrified, and he was smiling. "I'll see you in my office in a couple of weeks," he said, and with that, he turned and was gone.

There didn't seem to be any way I could avoid the inevitable. I was going to have to get up out of this bed and take that helpless infant and do what—I didn't know.

Soon nurses were bustling about packing my things, dressing the baby, bringing me a ton of free stuff—disposable diapers, formula, instruction books. *Aha! Instruction books! I'm saved. Somewhere in there will be a book that tells me what to do with this child.* I couldn't wait to go through the bag of goodies.

All too soon I was wheeled down to the car. The red-faced little stranger was placed in my arms, and in a matter of minutes we were home. I laid her down and started searching for the instruction book. Nothing in the free stuff. Maybe it was tucked in the blanket she was wrapped in. I searched. Nothing here either. Last resort—was it pinned to her diaper? Alas, nothing there either. We, her parents, were on our own. Somehow God—in His wisdom?—had seen fit to place this helpless infant in the hands of two untrained, unskilled people. He had trusted us with this helpless infant. He must have known what He was doing, we decided, and we'd just have to do the best we could. And so our parenting adventure began.

In my panic I had forgotten an instruction book that we always can turn to when in doubt. That book is the Bible. God usually has an answer to our dilemma. My family found what we were looking for in Deuteronomy.

> "And these words, which I am commanding you today, shall be on your heart; and you shall teach them diligently to your sons and shall talk of them when you sit in your house and when you walk by the way and when you lie down and when you rise up. And you shall bind them as a sign on your hand and they shall be as frontals on your forehead. And you shall write them on the doorposts of your house and on your gates."
>
> Deuteronomy 6:6–9 NAS

Let me paraphrase what this passage came to mean to us, because that is the essence of this book.

> "And these words, which I am commanding you today, shall be on your heart; and you shall teach them diligently to your sons and shall talk of them when you sit in your house playing games or watching TV or when you are working on a project or eating dinner together; and when you hike in the woods or through your city or neighborhood and when you lie down for a bedtime story and prayer time and when you rise up to get ready for work, school, or a family outing. And you shall keep them as close as your hand and impress them on your mind and on your children's minds. And you shall post them on your refrigerator door and on your front door."

Do you want your kids to believe what you believe—to share your value system? Do you want to see them pass down to their children the traditions and dreams that are precious, even sacred, to you? Do you want to raise them "on purpose"?

I believe the instructions God gave His people thousands of years ago are true foundation words for passing on values to our children— for raising our kids "on purpose."

Can you think of a better way to communicate your dreams, ideas, values, and beliefs than to spend time with and share your life with them? Evidently, God couldn't. That's why He encourages us to teach our children when we sit down with them, when we walk together, when we go to bed, and when we get up in the morning.

He also said to teach them *diligently*. The word *diligently* in this Scripture from Deuteronomy means "to sharpen a tool or whet a knife." In this case it means to bring a child to a keenness of reverence and knowledge of God. Bit by bit, as sons, daughters, fathers, and mothers play, work, and talk together, the child is honed to precision by the *diligent* values training of his/her parents.

It doesn't happen all at once—this sharpening of a child to know and accept your values—but each day he will come to know and understand a little better why his parents have certain beliefs and values.

Beginning early, as early as the day you bring your infant home from the hospital and continuing faithfully day in and day out, will help to avoid the alienation that often separates parents and their teenage children. There are no guarantees that someday you will not be alienated from your teen, but the chances are less likely if you know each other and share common goals and values.

Admittedly, the people to whom God addressed these words had a distinct advantage over us regarding spending time with their children. Opportunities were everywhere. The family, usually consisting of several generations, ate together and slept in the same room. Sons went to the fields with their fathers, and daughters learned necessary homemaking skills at their mothers' sides.

Later in the day fathers and sons returned to family compounds, where in the courtyard mothers, sisters, and grandmothers prepared a meal. It was a noisy, clamoring bunch of people who sat down on the ground around a mat or skin "table" to eat their dinner. Can you imagine the chatter, the stories, the laughter, the questions, and the teaching at those tables? Learning values was a natural outgrowth of family members sharing experiences.

Even bedtime was a group event. Everyone slept on a straw mat or rug in the single room of the house or on the rooftop in hot weather. Father, mother, children, and other family members lay down wherever they could find room.

Imagine the snores and wheezes, the turnings, the whispers, and giggles. Imagine negotiating your way in the darkness over that sleeping mass of humanity to comfort a whimpering child. But also consider the opportunities for teaching. Perhaps that day a small child had faced a temptation to take something that didn't belong to him. Still bothered over the episode, he might ask from his pallet, "Papa, why is it wrong to steal?" His father would answer by telling the story of how their ancestor, the great lawgiver Moses, received the commandments on top of a smoking mountain and of how God said, "You shall not steal." Father and child would talk about how stealing hurts both the one who steals and the one from whom an object is taken.

Our lives are very different from the ancients'. In our "modern" culture the children and parents no longer work side by side. We may miss each other at mealtimes, and we certainly don't sleep in the same room. Today in most families, the father is consumed by ten to twelve hours of commuting and working away from home. And in about sixty percent of modern families, mothers also go off to work. Overtaxed single parents head one-third of our households. For most exhausted parents it is just too hard to think about teaching their kids anything at the end of a workday. And as for mornings, forget it!

That's why I believe we must find other ways to impart our values to our children. In our family, we've done it primarily through recreation and play.

Most parents would benefit as much as their children if families made playing together a priority. When was the last time you deliberately played with your children? How long has it been since you took them to the circus or to the beach to hunt agates or shells?

Wouldn't you like to share a new experience with them, such as taking them to a nice restaurant for the first time and watching their eyes shine with excitement? As you and your child are having fun together, he will be learning how you think and react to life. He'll see you in the best and worst circumstances and learn what you value and what you don't.

When you take time to play and spend time with your children—doing something everyone in the family enjoys—values are learned painlessly and effectively.

Maybe you feel it's too late for your family. Your kids are teenagers now and they already are alienated from you. Let me assure you that they don't want to be. Kids want to be friends with their parents. It hurts them when they are not. Think back to a time when you and your children did things together that all of you enjoyed. Is there anything you could begin to do together again? Is there one topic you can discuss without a lot of judgment on both sides? Start there and begin to open and strengthen the lines of communication between you. It isn't hopeless; it just looks that way.

If we had it to do over, my husband, Ed, and I agree we'd raise our kids exactly the way we have—except we'd try to find even more time to play with them.

This practical manual will show you how to teach your children values by sharing your life with them. It's filled with ideas, instructions, and resources. It is my prayer that these pages will be a source of deep joy and fruitful experiences for you and your kids.

1

The Adventure Begins

" 'And now,' said Aslan presently, 'to business. I feel I am going to roar. You had better put your fingers in your ears.'

"And they did. And Aslan stood up and when he opened his mouth to roar his face became so terrible that they did not dare to look at it. And they saw all the trees in front of him bend before the blast of his roaring as grass bends in a meadow before the wind. . . .'"*

I paused to catch my breath. The only roaring we heard was the ocean in the distance. The canvas sides of our tent rattled, and the tent poles squeaked as a strong wind pounded our fabric house.

"Read, read, read!" two eager voices shouted in unison.

"Hey, wait, you two. I'm just trying to rest my voice," I told them.

Earlier that evening we'd intended to sit by the campfire and toast marshmallows, but the wind nearly had blown out the fire. Finally, we'd given up and crawled into our sleeping bags early. Now by the light of a flashlight, together we were sharing the adventure of reading *The Chronicles of Narnia* by C. S. Lewis.

As I turned the page and started to read again, the sound of the wind faded and we were once again in Narnia with Peter, Susan, Lucy, and Edmund, and a great lion named Aslan.

This was the first of hundreds of adventures my husband,

---

*C. S. Lewis, *The Lion, The Witch and the Wardrobe* (New York: Macmillan Publishing Company, Inc., 1961).

Ed, and I were to share with our two children over the next several years. Those adventures were planned "on purpose" as quality times—times when we could share our values with them.

It is possible for you, too, to communicate your values to your children through shared experiences. In this book I will show you how to do just that. I'll give you lots of ideas and tell you what happened when we used those ideas in our family. We had a lot of fun raising our kids, and you can have fun raising your kids, too.

Sharing Values Through Play

Ed and I really like to play—or maybe I should be honest and say that Ed understands the value of play, and he has spent our life together trying to teach me that value. Because I am a workaholic, I have to keep relearning its value on a daily basis.

I'm glad I've played as much as I have. I'm glad I learned to play for my own good, and I'm especially glad I learned to play with my children. When I think of the places we've been and the experiences we've shared together, my memories are very sweet. We've panned for gold in Montana, walked ocean beaches, and explored castles in Switzerland. We've camped on tops of mountains and in valleys, walked in the rain and blistering heat. We've been to ghost towns, hamlets, metropolises, and ancient walled villages.

We've been to zoos, game farms, and even encountered a bear in the wild. We've seen moose, deer, elk, beaver, mountain goats, game birds, otters, whales, trout, bald eagles, pikas, groundhogs, and hundreds of others of God's creatures. We've raced millipedes, seen the best figure skaters in the world, and ridden our bikes through lush, green forests. Sometimes we've spent a lot of money on a trip; more often we've spent almost nothing. It's a big beautiful world out there, and it's filled with interesting things to do—exciting adventures to share.

But these adventures rarely come looking for you. You have to determine to get out there and discover them with your children. It's not going to happen unless you set aside some time, plan where to go and what to do, and then get up and get going.

Because play is the way in which children learn best (it's their work), Ed and I decided early in our children's lives to spend time playing with them. We also decided we would find ways to instill our values in them whenever possible. Sometimes it would be verbal and intentional—like the time we took them to see the Constitution of the United States so that we could talk with them about the cost of freedom. We also realized that at other times their learning our values would be an outgrowth of just being with us. By letting them see how we acted and reacted, both positively and negatively (yes, negatively—we are so very human!), in all kinds of situations they would learn what we value and why.

Just being with your children will provide many opportunities to teach them spiritual values in a natural way. Once when we were camping in Mt. Rainier National Park, Mark, then about ten years old, was wearing a new pair of sandals to wade in the stream that flowed through the campground.

"Hey, Mom," he called, "I just lost my sandal."

"Oh, no!" I called back. "Those are brand new, and they weren't cheap. We'd better start looking for it."

Turning to our daughter, Wendy, I said, "Run downstream quickly and see if it's floating there."

Then I turned my attention back to Mark. "You, young man, start looking right here."

"I can't see very well; it's getting dark," he complained.

Soon the whole family was involved in the hunt. We shined a flashlight into the stream and fished around up to our armpits in the icy water to feel for a strap or a buckle.

"Well, I think it's gone," Ed sighed.

"Before we give up, let's pray," someone suggested.

So we prayed. "Dear Lord, please help us find that shoe. You know we can't afford another pair this summer. Thank You, Lord."

A few minutes later Ed called out, "I think I've got it. Here it is!"

He pulled out the sandal, which had been wedged between rocks.

Later in the evening, when we had warmed our frozen arms by the fire, we talked about the lost shoe, and we thanked God for helping us find it. Then someone remembered the story of the prophet Elisha. "Didn't one of the sons of the prophets lose an ax head in a stream?"

Ed opened the Bible and read us the story in 2 Kings 6:1–6. The man who lost the ax head was in great distress and cried out to Elisha, "What am I going to do, master? It was borrowed!" (*See* 2 Kings 6:5.)

Elisha asked to see the place where it had fallen. Then he cut down a stick, cast it into the stream at that location, and miraculously the iron ax head floated to the surface, where it could be retrieved.

After listening to the story, we compared it to our evening's experience, and it wasn't hard for the kids to see that God was the One who had helped us retrieve the lost shoe. That night they learned the practical value of prayer in a trying situation. And they learned it from us because we were there sharing the experience (unpleasant though it was) with them.

Spiritual values and priorities can be taught best in the course of everyday living, and wise parents learn to take advantage of these opportunities to teach spiritual lessons. Everyday events provide many opportunities for teaching about God's goodness, His provision, and the difference between right and wrong. In such situations the child learns in a natural, open way. He never feels as though he's getting a sermon.

"But I don't know what to do with my child," someone may protest. "I don't know *how* to play with him. I'm not even sure I'd *like* playing with him. What do a child and an adult have in common?"

You don't have to know very much to play with a child. The child is an expert at play; he'll teach *you*. Give any child some sunshine, water, and time, and he can amuse himself for hours. He will be happiest if you are there, too, helping him dam up the stream, laughing, talking, planning how to build the dam even bigger, and then plotting how you're going to "crash it down."

Play doesn't have to be elaborate or complicated. What the child wants is you and your undivided attention. He wants you to be there not only with your body, but also with your eyes, your heart, and yourself. You might fool some people into thinking you are paying attention to them, but you can't fool your child.

As you spend quality time with your children, you will have opportunities to find out what they're thinking, what false values they're picking up from their friends, and what problems they're encountering in their world. Some children don't share easily and need extended time with a parent before they're ready to open up and confide their deepest thoughts.

I know now what a good choice my husband and I made—the choice to spend lots of time playing with our children. For several years, Ed and I have been working with college students. I am startled by the large number of people we meet who scarcely know their parents because their parents were too busy to give themselves to their children. They were too busy teaching, working, cleaning, caring for others' needs—or perhaps even too busy serving the Lord—to spend quality time with their own kids.

One young man we knew said, "Sure, Dad always was there at all of my ball games. He always did the right thing and showed up, but he never was there with his heart."

He and other young people we've met saw right through their parents' perfunctory actions and right into their hearts. They knew all along that even while their parents were pretending to spend time with them, Dad was planning the next sales campaign and Mom was worried about the bills. Those young people wish they could go back in time and bat a ball with Dad or share an essay with Mom and know they had their parents' full attention. At the same time, these young people vow to raise their own children differently.

Some young people have found the way to get the parental attention they crave is by becoming very good at being very bad. A young woman we knew never could capture her parents', particularly her father's, full attention—until she became pregnant out of wedlock.

I never will forget the traumatic day I took the social worker to the hospital to pick up that baby when the young mother gave it up for adoption. I never will forget the tears the young mother cried. Nor will I forget the grandmother wrapping her tiny firstborn grandchild in the blanket she had made for her, bending to kiss the infant, and then turning and walking away. Oh, yes, the young woman *had* captured her parents' full attention.

When the school principal calls the parents to say the young person has been kicked out of school because he's using drugs, has been absent repeatedly, or has been in a fight, then he, too, finally has his parents' full attention.

A Changing World

We live in a world that is changing rapidly. Knowledge is exploding. Futurists estimate that society will increase its fund of knowledge by more than six times in the next 35 years. In our highly technological society, it's easy to feel lost and worthless. For many, life doesn't have much meaning. Working on an assembly line and screwing the same kind of screw into the same kind of panel for years has left these people wondering about the meaning of life. They've become cogs in a huge piece of machinery called "technology," and they've lost sight of the purpose for all of this progress.

Everywhere men, women, boys, girls, and young people are longing for meaningful relationships. Many single people run from one event to the next—from one singles' bar to another—looking for Miss or Mr. Right. Married people switch partners the way they change clothes. Boys and girls get new moms and dads frequently, and confused young people wonder if this is all there is to life.

The family is a tragic victim of this change. Family structure has changed from one mom, one dad, and children to a structure that includes multiple sets of parents, stepparents, grandparents, stepgrandparents, brothers and sisters, stepbrothers and stepsisters, plus all the aunts, uncles, and stepaunts and uncles. In describing this tangled web of relationships in families today, one writer gave the family structure a new name—"omnifamily." This blending of family units may happen not just once, but several times in a child's life. He may begin life with one set of parents and values, but go through life with several combinations of parents and several sets of values. No wonder confusion reigns!

We all are familiar with the loud uproar over the changing value system within our society, and particularly our schools. Today's value system is based on secular humanism, a man-centered, rather than God-centered, philosophy. This system proclaims that this world is the only one we can know, and that heaven and hell do not exist. It teaches that reason is the basis for truth; that man, not God, is the source of morals and values; and that we must work to improve the human condition. It is diametrically opposed to the Christian faith and would destroy Christianity if it could. Adherents to this system of thought believe that religion keeps people from progressing and that those who believe in God hold outmoded and antiquated values. They believe man's lot is improved by education, technology, and industry.

The pressure to conform comes from every direction. But we Christians must fight for our value system. We cannot allow the secular humanistic culture we live in to shape values for ourselves or for our children. Yes, technology and education are good. They have added much to our lives, but they are not the answer to all of man's problems. Religion does not keep people from advancing; religious ideas are not outmoded. Our children have to see that religion should have a place in their everyday lives. A relationship with Jesus Christ must be the focal point from which all other activities of life flow.

We must base our value system on the spiritual principles given in Scripture. In our rapidly changing culture it is important to have something absolute and irrevocable on which to tie our values, and that something is the Word of God. In our secular humanistic society we must identify Christian values for our family and live our lives within the guidelines of that value system.

The Family Is God's Idea

It also is important that we remember that the family was God's idea from the beginning. God intended the family to be an environment where children could be nurtured by both parents. A woman cannot be a dad, and a man cannot be a mom. Each parent gives to the child's life a perspective that the other cannot.

Sometimes today, often due to circumstances beyond our control, two-parent nurturing may not be possible. In some homes one parent may have abdicated the responsibility and walked out, leaving the remaining parent to cope as best possible. In other homes today's economic conditions often make it necessary for both parents to work, causing them to think more about survival than about nurturing their children.

In some cases, institutions, such as day-care centers and public and church schools, have assumed part of the children's care. We can be thankful for these institutions that provide physical care for children. But we must not expect them, excellent though many are, to provide our children with our value system.

Even if only one parent is in the home, even if both parents have to work, even if the child is placed in a day-care facility, it still is the parents' responsibility to teach their children right from wrong and to give them a value system. It is our responsibility as parents—and ours alone.

The exciting thing about passing your values on to your children is that it needn't be a hard task. It can be fun and very rewarding to share with your kids what is important in your life.

In our busy life-styles, we may never *find* time to share rich experiences with our children. We must *make* time for this important aspect of parenting. We must set aside quality time and commit ourselves to keeping that time as a sacred obligation. And when we do, much of what we want our children to know about our beliefs and value system will be passed along to them effortlessly. What better way to spend time with your children than to spend time playing with them—sharing experiences and building memories that no amount of money can buy?

This is not a book of instant success formulas. The truth is that even if you spend quality time with your child, there are no guarantees that everything will turn out exactly the way you hope. We all will face problems in raising our children. But we do know that the Word of God, firmly implanted in a child's life, never will be uprooted. It will become a part of him. Even though he may stray from God, he still knows what is true and good, and God can use it to bring him back again.

Even if your child seems to have thrown aside all you have taught him, you can be assured that underneath he knows your values. Somewhere down the road he will begin to reconsider what Mom and Dad believe.

As they grow older, most children will take the stuff of the values you have given them and rework it to fit their own needs and life-style. Someone has said that as a child begins to mature, he takes off the coat of values and beliefs you have made for him and unravels it to knit a garment of his own design. He doesn't throw away what you have taught him; he just adapts it to his own needs.

That's what is happening in our family. One of the greatest thrills of my life as a parent is watching our two grown children begin now, after a period of disdaining some of our ideas and values, to assimilate those same values and ideas into their life-style—changed, but still recognizable.

We can be sure of one thing. If we do our part in teaching our children, God faithfully will do His.

In the next chapter we will look at goals and priorities. With our overbusy schedules, how do we carve out time to share experiences with our children? What really is important? Is it a realistic goal to think we can spend quality time with our children?

2

What's Really Important?

The ferry cruised up to the dock and slid to a stop. We had come to Friday Harbor on Washington State's San Juan Island for one of our family's frequent three-day adventures to various nearby sites. Little did any of us know that this mini-vacation was to be a landmark time in our family.

We checked into our "motel," a log cabin set in a Douglas fir forest on an isolated beach. Once the fire was burning on the hearth, the little cabin became cozy and warm. The children, then eight and twelve years old, were delighted to find an old-fashioned pump organ, which they immediately began playing. They were so intrigued with the real moss chinking between the logs that they picked it out and neatly inserted it between the sheets on their parents' bed.

A brisk walk along the beach brought color to our cheeks, and soon we hurried to the cabin for supper. We ate, did dishes, and then revealed the real reason we had come. We were going to set goals and plan priorities for our family.

Ed handed each person paper and a pencil and instructed, "We want to set some goals for our family. I want to hear what you think our family should *do* and *buy* in the next few years. When we've finished we'll decide which one should be first, second, and so on. You can dream as big as you want. Nothing is too big, too far-out, or too silly. Who knows—maybe some of our wildest dreams will come true. First list all of our family's needs."

Everyone worked feverishly for fifteen or twenty minutes. Then Ed collected the papers and gave us another blank piece of paper. "Now let's write down all the things you'd like us to buy and all the things you wish we could do while we are living together as a family. This is a want list."

Again we worked industriously for about fifteen minutes. Then Ed collected the papers and began putting together the lists. As parents, we were pleasantly surprised by our children's generous attitudes. The lists looked something like this:

Needs List

Mark	Wendy	Ed	Gwen
Blender	Washer/Dryer	Retirement	Retirement
Car	Car	Redecorate	Roof
House Addition	Fence	Washer/Dryer	Fence
Retirement	College Fund	Shoes	Washer/Dryer
Washer/Dryer	Retirement	Fence	Redecorate
Dishwasher	Roof	Suit	Beds
College	Watches	Roof	Car
Redecorate	Freezer	Car	Shoes
	Shoes	Garden Window	Suit/Ed

Wants List

Typewriter	Sleeping Bag	College	Dishwasher
Bike	Trip/Europe	Sleeping Bags	Watch
Trip/Europe	Bike	Blender	Hawaii
Beds	Dishwasher	Trip/Europe	Trip/Europe
Organ	Suit/Ed	Bike	Blender
Hairdryer	Garden Window	TV Games	Bike
Calculator	Beds	Typewriter	Sleeping Bags

It is interesting now, ten years later, to look at those lists. Some of us thought certain items were necessities and others considered them wants. Now I see that so many of those dreams and wishes have come true and so many of those necessities have been purchased and almost worn out. Just recently we put up a new fence, but we never did get the TV games.

It is interesting to note that all of us had the same basic ideas about what we needed and wanted. Perhaps in some families the lists would vary more from person to person.

On everybody's list was the word *Europe*. This was our impossible dream—the ultimate goal for our family. We did not have enough money to vacation in Europe, and we had no hopes of ever getting that money, but dreams are dreams and goals are goals and in this session big dreams were allowed. (We finally did get to Europe, and later I'll tell you how.)

Goal setting—dreaming—is something every family should do, not just once, but throughout the years you are together as a family. This trip to Friday Harbor was the first of our many sessions for goal setting and priority planning.

Why Goals Are Important

Some school textbooks describe the family as any voluntary grouping of people living together. That's the extent of commitment of many modern families. It is so easy to lose sight of each other as we rush between meetings, ball games, ballet and music lessons, and myriad other activities—all good—all worthwhile—and all taking huge chunks of our time away from the family.

People who check in and out of the same house and share the same family name do not necessarily have a close family relationship and the same value system. If you want your children to share your values, then you must have common goals. Goal setting helps your children see what you value and why.

Prioritizing those goals and then setting a plan of action to achieve them can help your children learn how to accomplish their own goals.

Someone has said, "If you begin with a specific measurable goal, anything is possible." That is true if you have a plan that says "A" is more important than "B," and so we'll work on "A" first.

Goals help us to know how to spend our time and our money. How many parents have been sorry they bought some foolish toy for Christmas and two days later, it already is discarded or broken?

Have you ever considered buying your child an experience rather than a toy? No one ever can take the experience from him.

For many years, each Christmas season we tried to buy an experience for our kids. One year when they were very young, we took them to a Christmas breakfast a local department store holds in its dining room. Another year we took them to see *The Nutcracker*, their first exposure to ballet. And a third year we went to a live theater presentation of Dickens's *A Christmas Carol*. Not only were they wide-eyed with wonder at these experiences, but also they were being exposed to some of history's greatest classics.

They never have forgotten those Christmas adventure gifts. They are locked away in their minds—theirs to keep forever.

Gloria, a single mother of five, tells about buying her children a simple experience that they still talk about and treasure. It began when she took some vacation time and went home in the middle of a workday afternoon. Arriving unannounced, she told the kids to get in the car. Then she got behind the steering wheel and laid down the rules: No tattling on each other all day and no fights. They could choose anything they wanted to do, and she would provide the funds if at all possible.

They played together all afternoon—mother and children. She bought them helium-filled balloons and ice-cream cones. Someone wanted Chinese food so they had that for dinner. They went to the aquarium, and they went to the lake so the boys could chase frogs.

In the course of this spontaneous experience, those children learned that Mom could be a fun friend and that they were so special she wanted to spend a whole afternoon with them. They discovered that they probably don't need to fight as much as they do, and they learned that once in a while it is good to spend money on experiences that bring pleasure to everyone in the family.

Goals are important. They help you answer the question: "What do we want to accomplish as a family?" Some people I've talked with didn't set goals as a family and now, looking back, wish they had.

Goals help you to know whether you are making progress.

What a thrill it has been over the years to mark off areas of accomplishment on our family goal list. One of our children has finished college now, and the other one is just starting. And so far we've been able to pay the school bills, because college was an important goal for our family, and we planned for it.

Setting Goals

"Well," you might say, "it all sounds rather stuffy to me. Doesn't all that goal setting destroy any kind of spontaneity?"

Not at all. There is still plenty of room for spur-of-the-moment ideas and activities. Because our family knows what is important to us, we often drop what we are doing and rush to the top of a hillside in time to see a spectacular sunset. We have enjoyed early morning trips to a viewpoint to see an unusual alignment of planets and midnight excursions to see a meteor shower. If we hear about a display of northern lights—a rare occurrence which may last only a few minutes—you'll find us grabbing coats, scarves, and mittens, and heading for the door. Once we left the dishes on the table and headed for the locks between Lake Washington and Puget Sound to watch a huge Tudor mansion being moved by barge to a new location on the peninsula.

"That's crazy!" you might say. Well, maybe just a little. It's just that we value sunsets and moonlight, the first autumn rain, newborn kittens, and wonderful, unbelievable phenomena such as the undulating, draped curtains of the northern lights.

Goal setting does not destroy spontaneity. Instead it provides some structure to the happenings of your family life. When you know what is important to your family, then everything else takes its rightful place.

I think most of us will agree that family life in America today is a mess. Even families who have managed to survive without divorce are in many cases what that school textbook described—just a group of people voluntarily living in the same house. There is no cohesiveness of purpose. Setting some goals will help to bind together the family unit. You cannot work toward a common purpose (goal) separately. You must work together for a common purpose.

Your family goals will be different than ours and that's just fine. You probably will notice the lack of emphasis on sporting events in this book. It isn't that we don't like sports; we all do. We go to ball games as often as possible. We play organized games whenever we get the chance. But our children did not get involved in organized sports because they didn't have an aptitude for them and because in our area so many events are held on Sunday, and that warred against a higher goal in our family—involvement in church life.

But if sports activities are high on your family goal list—and they are in many families—and if you can be involved without sacrificing something more important, then sports are a good goal for your family. A child can learn much about commitment to a team and showing up regularly at practice to do his or her best.

Dick and Carol have four children. Two of the girls were interested in sports and the other two, a boy and a girl, were not. They attended every sporting event in which their athletic two participated. Carol says that the sporting arena provided a setting where they could express and display their values as parents—sometimes just by the way they reacted to a referee's bad call or a coach's unpopular decision. Their presence also let the child know that they were there to support her choice of activities. And it gave them a common ground for relating to the child.

Gloria, my single friend, says that once her boys join a team she won't let them drop out, even if they want to because the coach won't play them. She says they're learning the discipline of trying their hardest no matter what happens.

Marg says that her son, too, spent a great deal of time on the bench, but she and her husband were there anyway. Later she taught him and her other three children to play tennis—her first love.

She taught them because she valued the game and wanted them to share her love of the sport. Her children, like Gloria's, learned that mother can be a lot of fun. She talked, too, about the open communication that developed between them when they played together.

Marg thinks that as you get to know your children and they get to know you through the avenue of play, they will then be more willing to accept your other values—such as spiritual values.

You won't reach all of your goals. We haven't. Life's too short and goes by too quickly. But that's all right. Nobody who sets goals reaches all of them.

Recently I read about a company that annually presents a failure award to a person who had a great idea that didn't work. This award's purpose is not to berate the recipient, but to encourage people to pursue ideas—even if they might not work.

The exciting reality is that you will reach some of your goals, and many more than if you had not set any. You will become family achievers. When our daughter, Wendy, walked across the stage and received her diploma from the president of her college, we all felt the achievement, because it takes commitment to a goal and sacrifice on the entire family's part to make such dreams come true.

Dreams can come true, but first you have to dream.

Behavior and Goals

In goal setting it is important that we not analyze ourselves to death. Continual reevaluation can become navel gazing, and instead of motivating our families, can cause them to stand still. Nobody wants to be reminded seventy-five times a day that he can't do that because it isn't part of the family goals.

Rather, goal setting is the structure upon which we hang our family life. It is possible to spend so much time planning and evaluating that it becomes a cop-out to living. That's not the idea I am trying to express here.

One helpful activity is to think about those things which war against your goals. What keeps you from successfully achieving quality family time? May I suggest some possibilities gleaned from my own experience?

Television can be a real enemy of family goals. It can consume so much time that there isn't much left for working on goals. I think every home should have a television; it's a window to the world. But we should control its usage if we are determined to spend quality time with our families.

Overwork also can war against goals. We've all heard about the corporate father who disappears into the newspaper at the end of the day and then falls asleep on the sofa right after dinner. But corporate fathers are not the only ones guilty of overwork. Mothers are guilty too. Women who are trying to hold down at least two jobs, a career and full-time homemaker, certainly have a reason to feel overworked—they are.

Mothers, is it really necessary for you to work? Could you reach your goals if your life-style were less hectic? If your goals were different would one income be enough? Could you get by with a part-time job?

"She doesn't understand," you probably are saying now. Yes, I think I do understand. Many of you have no choice, and it is tough. I don't have all the answers about how to juggle work and home. I'm a working mother, too, and I have the same struggles you do. I'm too busy, and I get too tired. I did wait until the children were older before I returned to work. That helped some.

What I do know, because I've been there, is that even though I was at home for many years as a full-time homemaker, I still overworked and cheated my family. They got leftover Mom too many times. Overwork is a real enemy of family life—an enemy we need to fight.

Too many activities outside the home war against goals. The choice of activities in which a family can participate is so mind-boggling that I won't attempt to enumerate them here. You must decide which of your activities are important to your family and which goals need to be sacrificed to make family goals attainable.

When our children were young, one of our goals was to spend one night at home together each week. We decided to keep that "family night" as a covenant to each other. No one could be absent unless the entire family agreed that what the person wanted to do was more important than the family night. Even then we attempted to reschedule. Later we will talk more about how to set up a family night and how to ensure its success. I honestly can tell you that the sacrifices were worthwhile. We all look back on those nights as having provided some of our finest memories.

We can become victims of our lack of goals. We can drift from one activity to another—never coming close to the important things we'd like to see happen in our families. What choices are you making as a family? The goals you achieve will be affected by the choices you make along the way.

Achieving Goals

If you never have read a book on goal setting, let me encourage you to do so. Here I will touch on some of the basic principles related to goal setting.

1. Set specific goals. It will not do to say, "This year we will spend more time together as a family." That is too general. Rather, your goals should be: "On Sunday afternoon we will walk to the park with a bag of bread for the ducks, and we will talk about how God has equipped the duck for his life-style."
2. Set measurable goals. The more specific a goal, the more measurable it will be. After Sunday afternoon's excursion to the duck pond, you will know whether you have achieved your goal. It is all right to have a general goal, such as spending more time together this year. But without many measurable goals throughout the year, you never may know if you succeeded in spending more time together.
3. Make your goals attainable. Nothing is as discouraging as unattainable goals. An example of a goal that would have been unattainable in my family is: "We'll spend quality time together, and the kids will not fight." Maybe you can make that happen at your house, but it was unrealistic for us.
   An attainable goal is: "We'll spend time together, and if the kids balk or fight, we'll work it out as best we can. Perhaps they will learn something about relating to others in the family or settling differences."
4. Tailor your goals for your family. I already have given you many ideas about teaching values through shared experiences, and I've told you a number of activities we did together as shared experiences. You will read about many more activities in the pages of this book. But remember that our family goals may not be right for your family. Only your family can decide what's important to you.

5. Pursue your goals one day at a time. Begin today to work on your goals. If one of your goals is to spend quality time with each child every day, then begin tonight at bedtime. Give that child your undivided attention for ten minutes. Listen to what he has to say. Listen to what he's *not* saying; that may be just as important. Pray with him about his fears, his concerns, and his joys.

   If you have three children you will spend 30 minutes of your day in a very positive manner. You still will have twenty-three-and-a-half hours to do what you need to do.
6. Ask yourself: "Is this goal important enough to give it five minutes of my time today?" If you answer "yes," then give it priority time. If you answer "no," then it's time to reevaluate the goal. Maybe the goal just isn't important to you. If that is the case, then drop that particular goal.

The Rewards

The rewards of goal setting are many. It may be years before you realize these rewards. A closeness develops among family members who are united around a common purpose.

You will experience great joy at seeing your children adopt your value system. You may not know the full extent of that adoption until they have their own children. Then you will be able to say with the Psalmist: "Great is the Lord and most worthy of praise; his greatness no one can fathom. One generation will commend your works to another; they will tell of your mighty acts. They will speak of the glorious splendor of your majesty, and I will meditate on your wonderful works" (Psalms 145:3–5 NIV).

What's really important? My answer to that question is knowing who you are as a family, and deciding what is going to have first place in your family life. That's what's important!

3

Planning the Time

"Where are we going, Dad? Where are we going?" Mark asked with excitement.

"I can't tell you, son. It's a surprise," Ed told the bouncing young boy.

"But, Dad, I want to know."

"No, Mark, you just will have to trust me."

It was family night at our house, and this particular evening we had planned an event around the subject of trust. Earlier in the evening we had read the Scripture passage about Abraham following God without knowing where God would lead him.

"Oh, all right. What do we have to do?" continued Mark's mild complaint.

"First let's get into the car," Ed replied, glancing up at the night sky. "Hmmm. Kind of cloudy and rainy out here. I don't know how this adventure will work. Well, we'll just have to see."

Half an hour later we reached the University of Washington campus. We walked together across the parking lot to a tall, domed tower. One night each month the university opened its observatory to the public for a few hours. Ed had clipped an article about this service from the newspaper and had filed it for future reference. We climbed the stairs to the tower, and hoped for a break in the clouds—even a tiny break—so we could get a glimpse of the full moon and night sky. But after standing around for quite some time, we realized that the clouds were not going to part.

"Some adventure, huh, Dad?" Mark nudged Ed with his elbow.

"Say," said the attendant. "Would you like to come to the theater and see some slides of solar eclipses around the world? You know this area of the country will experience a total eclipse of the sun in a few weeks."

"What do you say, kids? Shall we go?" Ed asked.

"Might as well," Wendy said. "We don't have anything else to do."

So we listened to the attendant's highly informative and very interesting presentation about solar eclipses. Because no one else was in the theater, we had the attendant's undivided attention and asked many questions.

Little did Ed and I realize that our adventure at the observatory would create in our children a great interest in astronomy. Several years later, we visited another observatory in Goldendale, Washington, and finally were treated to a spectacular view of the moon, Venus, Jupiter, and beautiful Saturn.

One of Wendy's favorite posters, purchased at yet another observatory, in Colorado, is a beautiful pink nebula in Serpens called NGC 6611, Messier 16. And all of this interest in astronomy began when Ed clipped an article and filed it for reference.

Planning Is Vital

Planning is a vital part of teaching our children our values through shared experiences. We have to plan to spend time with them. We have to plan the time we spend with them, and we have to plan what values we want them to acquire through the experience. If we fail to plan, other commitments swallow the time we should be giving to our family.

Making no plan is a plan in itself: a plan to fail at spending time with the most important people on earth—our family. Busy fathers and mothers must write "Special Appointment" across an evening, a day, or a week, and then keep that special appointment as if it were a sacred obligation. It is. I can assure you that twenty years from now you never will remember what other things you *could have done* on those evenings given to your family, but none of you ever will forget what you *did*.

Planning for shared adventures begins to falter when no one in the family takes it on as a special assignment. Someone who enjoys the task should be responsible. In our family, it is Ed. I have accused him of having more fun planning than actually doing an activity.

If no one in your family enjoys planning, you can make the planning itself a family event. Remember that planning takes time. This means that the individual or the family doing the planning must block out another segment of time for planning. Take an evening or a weekend afternoon and make a tentative plan for the next six months. Get a calendar and start filling in dates with family activities.

Much can be learned from the give and take involved as people discuss their ideas and wishes about having fun. Probably the first thing learned is that somebody has to give in to the ideas of others, at least some of the time. Before your planning session it would be wise to lay some ground rules such as: "Nobody calls anybody else's idea 'stupid' " and "everybody has to suggest one idea sometime during the evening."

Research Your Plan

Where *does* one find ideas about activities to do in his area? I know this is a problem because parents often ask us where they can hike that won't be too strenuous for a five-year-old child, or what inexpensive event could nine- to twelve-year-old children do for a birthday party. And usually we have an idea to share, or we can look in our files for further suggestions. (More about files in a minute.)

One source of local activities is the library. Most libraries are filled with regional publications: books, pamphlets, maps, and much more material. Ask your librarian to show you the regional section, and then write down those things which catch your attention.

Another helpful section in the library is the travel section. If your planning will take you beyond your region, you should spend time investigating this section. There you will find books with travel ideas for all budgets—from backpacking to the most elegant hotels and restaurants.

Often the library has a stack of pamphlets and folders about current events in your city. Ask to see these. The library itself may have a full schedule of events such as puppet shows, movies, story hours, and special guests. Get a printed schedule of these events.

Use the library. It is crammed with information, and it is free.

Visit the local chamber of commerce. It, too, will have a list of local and regional events, and who knows what else you might find? Most people never fully explore their own neighborhoods, cities, counties, and regions. There is probably more to do within a ten-mile radius of your home than you could accomplish in a month of leisure time.

Bookstores are a treasure-trove of information and ideas. Spend an afternoon browsing the shelves with your kids. Again, focus on the regional publications and travel books. Buy a few; they are a choice investment in your family's future. Incidentally, you are not only gathering information about places to go and things to do, but you also are teaching your children to value books and how to find information on a given topic.

On our shelves are well-worn books describing hiking trails, interesting architecture, restaurants, shops, hotels, arts, sports, sights, and short tours in the Puget Sound region. You will find more books about your own area than you can afford to buy.

Once you have purchased the books, it is time to face the fact that all the books in the world won't do you any good unless you take time to read them. Read books not only for ideas of places to go, but also to gather a historical background about the places you will visit.

One summer we found ourselves tramping across Oregon to explore seashore, mountains, mining camps, ghost towns, and more. A helpful book called *Oregon for the Curious* added interesting historical perspectives to many of the sites we explored.

Reading also can give you a background for other kinds of activities, such as cultural events. Before either of our children reached junior high school, I decided it would be helpful if they were exposed to some Shakespeare. Most young people have to study Shakespeare in school, and most of them hate it.

Ed and I decided to take the kids to the Shakespearean

Festival in Ashland, Oregon. We very carefully selected the plays, because our intent was not to frighten them or expose them to more mature material than they could handle.

Then we began to plan the trip. One of the things I did was to go to the library and find a book containing Shakespeare's plays in simplified English. During our trip we read these in the car and also at night around the campfire. This book helped the kids to understand the plays, and helped me to update my knowledge of Shakespeare's work.

When we finally sat in the Elizabethan outdoor theater, Mark, then about eight years old and a real wiggler, sat spellbound on the edge of his seat for the entire performance. He understood and was interested in what was happening on the stage.

During the next couple of years, Wendy and Mark watched Shakespearean plays on public television while holding an open copy of *The Complete Works of Shakespeare* on their laps.

The end result was that both of them shocked their teachers with their knowledge of Shakespeare. And last summer it was thrilling to sit with Wendy in a theater in Stratford-upon-Avon in England and watch *Macbeth*. We sat in the front row, and we didn't miss a word of what was said.

Regional magazines are an excellent source of information about places to see and things to do in your area. Most Sunday papers have a magazine section containing local activities and interests. The travel section of the newspaper also has information about upcoming events in your city. Our local weekend paper has a "What's Up?" section listing everything from area garage sales to dog shows. Many national magazines also have a regional section brimming with all kinds of interesting information.

What about the yellow pages? Our phone book lists dozens and dozens of travel agencies, and all of them have someone sitting at the other end of a phone line just waiting for your call. They can help you with travel plans—from taking a Greyhound bus to a nearby city to flying to Europe on the Concorde.

Don't overlook another important source—your friends and acquaintances. Make it a practice to ask people what they like to do when they have some free time. Where do they like to go? Ask them about their favorite restaurant in your area, and ask them why they enjoyed it so much. Ask them about their favorite free activities in your area.

Every time you ask friends for their ideas you probably will learn something you didn't know. The people with the best ideas are those who enjoy doing things—those who don't mind putting forth some effort to be active. Don't expect good ideas from people who spend their Saturdays watching television.

Resources for Planning

Probably enough adventure ideas to fill a book already have passed through your hands. Perhaps in the newspaper you read an article about a place you would like to see. But instead of taking action, you folded the paper, laid it down, and forgot all about it.

Our trip to the observatory happened because Ed saw the article in the paper, tore it out, and put it in a file folder. Collecting adventure ideas takes some effort, but it's well worth it.

The best place to organize information is a file. A filing system doesn't have to be elaborate, but it is essential to have some system for keeping track of information. All you need are some file folders and a cardboard box to hold them.

We have about 150 file folders labeled with places to go and things to see. Let's pick one at random and see what's in it. How about "Florida"? Hmmm. The file contains a lot of information I brought home from my last business trip to Florida. There's airline information, pamphlets about St. Augustine, Vizcaya, and The Keys. Here's a pamphlet about a London Fog coat outlet in Florida. And here's some more information about outlet centers. Maybe this will be a great trip after all.

Here's an article clipped from *USA Today:* "Orlando unlimited: Fun doesn't stop with Disney." It lists eleven attractions in addition to Walt Disney World. The file contains more about Central Florida. Did you know there is a cartoon museum only three miles from Orlando's airport? Did you know you can take a sunrise balloon ride over Cinderella's Castle and the surrounding area?

And here is an article suggesting what to do when your money runs out—visit the Tupperware World Headquarters. The last pieces in this file folder are two *Southern Living* magazine articles about Florida and a clipping that lists an 800 number to call for help with reservations.

I think, after looking into this folder, we're about ready for a trip to Florida.

The secret to having plenty of information when you pursue an adventure is to gather that information in advance. Write for free travel information, or let your kids clip and mail the travel coupons in magazines. They'll be helping you, and they'll enjoy receiving the information in the mail. Your problem will be getting them to part with the brochures so that you can file them.

Train yourself to watch for ideas, and then clip them out on the spot. Probably someone will complain about the hole in the newspaper or magazine, but that someone will forgive you when you have just the right information when it is needed in the future.

There are several ways to file information. You can file by location or by family interests. Filing by location is easy to understand, but let me explain how to file by interests.

If your family is interested in antique cars, start collecting information about antique car shows and displays. Put all that information together in the same file folder, regardless of the geographic location of the article.

Whatever is your family's special interest, watch for information about that subject. If it's ice cream, watch for information about ice cream. Tear it out and file it in your "Ice Cream" folder. Then when you have a yen to go someplace unusual for ice cream, you can pull out the information you need.

(Eating ice cream is not my particular passion, but a friend took us to a restaurant in Jackson, Michigan, where root beer floats are served in foot-high crystal vases and a standard sundae has about ten scoops of ice cream.)

Another way to file information is by subject. Here are some possible headings to start you thinking about your file:

Nature
Botany: Regional plants.
Marine life: If you live near the sea.
Wild animals in your area
Birds: Some people make a lifelong hobby of watching birds.
Astronomy: You already have heard our story.

Mechanized Transportation

Trains: Schedules to the nearest towns. If your children never have ridden on a train, plan to take them.

Model trains: We have two very fine clubs in our area which love to have visitors. It's amazing to see the amount of time and energy grown men put into playing with trains.

Airplanes: Airports and air museums are fascinating places for kids.

Trucks: Visit a local dispatcher or a truck terminal and watch how truckers handle the big rigs. Maybe you'll be able to ride in the cab of a truck.

Communications

TV stations usually will allow visitors. Watch for information.

Radio stations: Let your children see the announcers and disc jockeys they hear on the air.

Telephone companies may offer occasional tours of their facilities.

History

The Sunday paper: History seems to be a favorite topic for newspaper writers.

State parks often are built on historical sites. Write to your state park system for information.

Tours of old homes and buildings are offered annually by many societies. Watch for the announcements in the newspapers.

Regional publications such as *Sunset* in the West and *Southern Living* in the South often include information about historical events and places.

Science

Science centers have many events geared for children and young people.

Universities offer science programs which are open to the public. Call their offices, make notes of their programs, and file them.

Drama

Seasonal events are fun. *A Christmas Carol* is performed annually in our area.

Many city parks stage theatrical performances. Check the newspaper.

Investigate small theaters in your area. Some may be children's theater.

Arts

Ballet: Expose your children to ballet. The *Nutcracker* is a delightful story, and is performed annually in many cities.

Opera: This can be fun for the whole family—if it is sung in English and if everyone knows the story before the singing begins.

Art galleries usually have permanent and some changing exhibits.

Government

Many *government buildings* are open for touring. Once my two children and I toured our state capitol in Olympia, Washington. Our tour guide said, "I usually don't do this, but because the group is small I think I'll take you to the top of the dome." We crawled up a narrow, winding staircase and stepped onto the portico on the top of the dome. I doubt that many people in our state have been to the top of our capitol's dome.

Courts of law are interesting places to visit and in most cases can be viewed when court is not in session.

Police stations and fire stations also are open for tours. Call them and find out their schedules.

Industry

Candy factories welcome guests. You'll have to make arrangements to tour the larger ones. Most have a seconds (rejects) shop that will make them a favorite stop for your family.

Pulp mills

Woolen and cotton mills

All kinds of factories, both large and small.

Agriculture

Dairy farms
Farms where you can pick fruit and vegetables.
Horse ranches: Visit the blacksmith shop.
Research farms

Cultural

Folk festivals
Ethnic food fairs
Native American events

Planning to Have Fun and Not Spend Much Money

When we were pastoring a small church in California, we drove to nearby Sacramento to enjoy an inexpensive adventure. I don't remember what it was, but I know it was inexpensive. We had virtually no money. I remember that on the way home we stopped at a gas station, put a handful of coins into a vending machine, and bought something we didn't need—candy! It was the best candy I ever had tasted.

During those very lean years we still had fun adventures together. We probably have visited every free zoo on the West Coast. We've been to art galleries and museums. We've toured state parks and seen big trees and more big trees—sequoias, redwoods, cedars, and Douglas firs.

We've picked up sand dollars, driftwood, and agates on the beaches. We've splashed in hot springs and scores of waterfalls.

None of these adventures cost us one dime. They were free for the taking. It did require some planning, some time, and some effort to include all these things in our family's adventure scrapbook. Later in this book is a whole chapter of ideas for family adventures.

Mapping Out the Plan

Let's suppose you found something of interest in your file—an adventure you want to pursue. Now it is time to plan the event. The following checklist will help you:

1. Who's going on this adventure? Mom? Dad? Dad and one child? Mom and a child? Who?
2. How far away is it?
3. What time do you need to leave?
4. What kind of clothing is appropriate?
5. Do you need to take a lunch?
6. How much money will you need?
7. Is there enough gas in the car?
8. If it is a ticketed event, have you bought the tickets?
9. Where are they?
10. How long will you be gone?
11. Will you need to eat a meal on the road or in a restaurant?
12. What will you do on the way?
13. What favorite toy, blanket, or pillow should be taken so there are no tears later because it is missing?
14. Have you done some background reading? Don't forget the book so that you can share what you've learned when you arrive.

The checklist is completed. You're ready to launch.

Planning What to Do on the Way to the Event

I don't know how it is in your family, but in ours, closed car doors signaled the beginning of a battle in the backseat. One of my two fought by mouth, and the other with feet.

In self-defense I started reading to them in the car—even for the twenty-minute ride to church on Sundays. But on a long trip my strained vocal cords begged for rest. For each child we usually brought a small dishpan filled with whatever small books, toys, puzzles, or coloring books each had chosen. I recall the hot summer day in California when I found a brightly colored coagulated mass that once had been color crayons and now was worked securely into the carpet in the back of the car. That day lives in my memory right up there with the time I found a sock filled with crayons—only after it had been in the dryer for forty minutes.

Sleep is a very good thing for little people to do when traveling. Bring along favorite pillows, toys, and blankets. You'd better decide how much you want older children to sleep unless you don't mind them watching late-night television in your motel while you try to sleep.

When Plans Go Wrong

Not all plans work out as expected. Earlier I mentioned a full solar eclipse that was predicted for our area. This event may happen only once in a lifetime, and our family waited expectantly for the day to arrive.

As the day of the eclipse neared, local newspapers and television stations instructed us how to view the eclipse without damaging our eyes.

We had prepared our viewing tubes, and done our research. We planned to travel ninety miles south to where the eclipse would be total. But early that February morning we awoke to the Northwest's worst pea soup weather conditions. It looked absolutely hopeless.

In addition, just a day before the eclipse, Ed and I had comforted a young friend's widow when he died. His death was traumatic for both of us, and our sorrow was real.

We assessed the weather, our sorrow, the distance to travel, and decided to cancel this adventure. We decided to watch the eclipse on television instead. Imagine our dismay when we learned that the weather had cleared miraculously for a few minutes, and everyone who had gone to that location had a perfect view of the eclipse.

The best plans do go astray sometimes. You can't do much about that, except possibly to have an alternative plan. It may not be your first choice and may not be quite as exciting, but having an alternative plan will help to take the sting out of losing the first adventure. Some of our most memorable adventures began when a prior plan failed. Be prepared to regroup and head in another direction.

I've said it before, but it bears repeating: We can't teach our children our values unless we spend quality time with them, and quality time must be planned. Block out time on the calendar, gather the information, do the research so that you know what you are experiencing, file research information where you can find it, and bring your children into your planning process. If the plan fails, regroup and do something else.

Now that our children are grown, we realize that in addition to spending time with us to learn our values, they also learned how to plan. Mark recently planned a trip to Europe with a friend. Our daughter, who is a youth minister in Belgium, plans all kinds of events for the young people in her church.

Everyone in our extended family knows about "the file" and often the phone will ring and someone will say, "Uncle Ed, you know that place you told me about? Could I have the telephone number?" Someone has said that planning eliminates the "if only" syndrome. If only we had gone there. If only we had taken more time with the kids. If only we had saved for that one special vacation. Planning brings the future into the present so that we can do something about it.

If we take the time to plan our adventures carefully we will reap the full benefit of shared experience with our children, and they will learn what we treasure and value in our lives.

4

Curiosity: The Door to Adventure

"Grandma, where does the moon go in the daytime?"

"It doesn't go anywhere, Mark. Sometimes you can see the moon in the daytime, and sometimes it's on the other side of the earth."

"Is there really a man in the moon?"

"Not really."

"Could I ever live on the moon?"

"Maybe someday."

"Grandma, do I ask too many questions?"

At last Grandma stopped what she was doing and looked at him. "No, Mark, you don't ask too many questions. That's how you learn."

With that, the questions began again.

The Age of Curiosity

When that exchange took place, Mark was four years old—at the prime of the questioning age and a master at asking questions.

All of childhood is a time of curiosity, but the peak time of curiosity is the period between ages three and five. If you don't have one in your own household, borrow a three-year-old child for the afternoon. Follow him around and watch him. He will feel things, poke his finger into things, lick things, jump on and off things, pull on things, and if you leave him alone long enough, he will produce absolute chaos.

He will ask questions and more questions. Research shows that three-year-old children ask more than three hundred questions a day. They ask questions for many reasons. They ask to gather information. "What's that?" they'll ask, pointing to a dog. They ask to learn how to ask questions. They ask to try to deal with some underlying fear: "Will you still be my mommy when I'm grown up?" They ask to try to separate the real world from fantasy: "Did King Kong really live?" And they ask questions to practice asking questions and answering them themselves: "Where are you going today? I know, you're going shopping."

Parents' Role in Curiosity

Encourage It

Create an atmosphere where questions are allowed and encouraged. Research shows that curious, questioning children are better equipped emotionally and intellectually than the less curious. They do better in school, are generally quicker at solving problems, and are more flexible and creative.

Children naturally are curious, so encouraging curiosity isn't difficult. Think about the infant who is learning to crawl. Mother continually is taking strange things out of the crawler's mouth. But it is through his mouth that he learns about hardness and softness, cold and heat, wet and dry. Everything goes into the mouth because that is how he satisfies his curiosity about an object—at least for a while.

One day I discovered Wendy chewing something strange and began to investigate. Not to worry, Mom. It was just some garden snails—shells and all. Another time I found Wendy and our small dog chewing on a bacon rind the dog had brought home.

This time of curiosity can be a dangerous time for the child, and it is important to provide safety while still allowing him, within reason, to investigate his surroundings. It is best to remove anything that is unsafe from the reach of crawlers and toddlers.

My strategy was to fill lower drawers and cabinets with plastic containers and lids, pots and pans, and canned goods.

In fact, I still do out of habit although we no longer have little people at our house. Very soon the toddlers learned that the drawer with the plastic containers was theirs, and they could open it and take everything out—and they usually did several times a day. If they opened the other lower cupboards or drawers they could play with the canned goods or pots and pans, and no harm was done.

Little ones of this age like to fit things together, stack things up, pull things—off if possible, put small things into bigger things, crumble things, smell things, and of course, taste other things.

They are maximizing the use of all of their senses and abilities to discover their world. Oh, that we all could retain the curiosity of a child! So many adults have dulled senses. We eat, but we really don't taste anything. We smell the roses, but the fragrance doesn't penetrate our brain. We see colors, but they are just colors. We feel softness, coolness, sharpness, moistness, and dryness, and it means nothing to us because we are so used to the sense of touch. We hear birds' songs, yet we don't really hear them; it's just birds chirping. If we could become more aware of our world, as children are, how much more alive and interesting we would be.

No matter what the child's age—infant, toddler, elementary-school child or older—parents need to encourage, not stifle, curiosity. By allowing and encouraging curiosity, you grow creative people; curiosity is the seedbed of creativity.

When we first moved to Washington State, our house had an empty lot behind it. The lot was filled with trees, berry vines, and bushes. It was autumn when we arrived, and most of the bushes had fruit on them. When we explored the woods for the first time, Mark pointed to a blackberry and asked, "Can I eat this?" I recognized the berry from a childhood visit to Washington State. So we started sampling the blackberries. Then Mark pointed to a small red berry. "Can I eat this?" he asked.

"I don't know, Mark," I said. "I'm not sure. It isn't a good idea to taste things if we don't know whether they're safe to eat. But I'll find out as soon as possible."

His curiosity sparked that of the rest of the family, and we began to study about wild edible foods. We discovered that the red berries Mark had found were red huckleberries, which can be cooked into a delicious jelly. In our woods we also found a small, round, dark berry called salal which tastes sweet when eaten off the vine, but makes terrible jelly. We learned that Oregon grape is as sour as anything can be, and discovered a foul-smelling fruit called swamp current. We also learned to identify several varieties of blackberries: Himalayan blackberries, Evergreen blackberries, and—best of all—a little one that runs on the ground on a thorny vine.

Later in our investigation we ate young cattails which taste something like corn. They are cooked, buttered, and eaten like corn on the cob, and when you finish you have an interesting plateful of cobs which resemble knitting needles.

We also learned to enjoy lamb's-quarters, a weed that springs up between the garden's rows of spinach and Swiss chard, and has more nutritional value than either of them. By the time we had finished our investigation, we also had eaten violet leaves, miner's lettuce, blackcap raspberries, blueberries, huckleberries, salmonberries, wild raspberries, thimbleberries, chickweed, watercress, and dozens of other plants.

As we learned about wild edible plants, we began to search for them. Both Mark and Wendy became proficient at identifying plants and berries, and it soon became impossible to hike with them during the summer months because they spent all their time foraging for food.

If we had not responded to Mark's curiosity, all of us would have missed out on the adventure of learning about this region's wild edible plants. We had to become as curious as he was.

Curiosity can lead your family through one adventure after another. Curiosity is the perfect tool for bringing together a family around a shared experience. It would have been fun to learn about all those things on my own, but it was a dozen times more fun to share the adventure as a family.

Parents need to remember what it is like to be curious. They need to encourage curiosity, and they need to participate in their children's curiosity. They need to continue to have a childlike desire to learn about everything.

Stimulate It

Let's return to the three-year-old child. He's as curious as he can be. You can spend the day taking things out of his hands, pulling him down from places he doesn't belong, or—as we once had to do because our attention shifted for a moment and one of our children decided to taste paint thinner—making a quick dash to the emergency room.

Instead of spending all your time saying "no" or "don't," provide children with tactile, sensory experiences that allow their curiosity to flourish. Regardless of the children's age, toddler or older, we need to provide them with an environment which stimulates their curiosity.

Let them play in the cookie or bread dough. They're dying to know what it feels like. And why don't you get in there and squeeze the dough through your fingers with them? Let them hold a newborn chick, and then you take your turn. Rub its soft down under your nose, and watch your children's eyes when you do. Let them smell the earthy scent of mushrooms, the tang of lemon peel, and the once-smelled, never-to-be-forgotten aroma of candy canes.

Provide them with blunt scissors and an old catalog so they can cut out the pictures. Let them splash in water and blow soap bubbles. Take your child to a hillside and blow the biggest bubbles ever seen. (If you add a little glycerin to the soapy water, it makes stronger bubbles. Use a huge ring, like a rounded-out coat hanger, to make bubbles. The really big rings make really big bubbles. The record is twenty-four feet across.) The children will learn all kinds of wonderful things from these experiences, and so will you. And all of you will have shared in the adventure of curiosity.

Maybe your children are no longer toddlers, but are in school. And maybe you never have considered using curiosity as a tool for family adventure. I suggest that you take a half-hour walk together and agree that you will ask questions about everything you see. Take a pad and pencil to record what is spotted. Then promise each other that you will learn the answers to your curiosity questions.

Let me tell you some curiosity items Ed and I discovered recently during a half-hour walk. We parked the car at a small lake, and walked across the parking lot. "What's that?" I asked, pointing to a large wooden ball hanging in a display area.

"I don't know," Ed said. "I've never seen anything like that before."

We walked over, read the display, and discovered that this two-foot diameter ball had been used in logging competitions in the past. Instead of the usual logrolling contests with which we are familiar, the early loggers stood on and rotated this ball as it floated in the water. They certainly increased that activity's level of difficulty by using this ball rather than a cylindrical log. Staying upright while spinning a log would be difficult enough, but this seemed almost impossible.

A few feet farther down the trail we spotted notches cut in the huge tree stumps. We knew what these were because shortly after moving to this area where logging has always been done, we had asked and answered the same questions.

The notches are where early loggers fitted a plank into the huge cedars and fir trees they were sawing down by hand with double crosscut saws. They stood on the planks, sometimes ten to fifteen feet above the ground, and sawed away. When they removed the planks, there were the notches in the trunks, silent reminders of the rigors of logging before power chain saws.

Just a little farther down the trail we stopped to admire the pattern of colored fall leaves floating in a swampy pond. We also noticed many little black creatures with four legs and long tails swimming in the murky water. We decided they must be salamanders.

Then a bird cried out with a loud call—one I didn't recognize. It flew from a clump of swamp grass, but I didn't get to see it. I still wonder what kind of bird it was.

The final curiosity on this short walk was bubbles rising from the floor of the lake. What caused those bubbles? We decided the cause might be decaying vegetation deep down in the muck of the lake bottom.

We discovered five curiosity items about which we could learn more during a thirty-minute walk. Curious people are aware of their surroundings. They want to know more than they know. They haven't yet lost all of their three-year-old child's curiosity. They want to know why, where, what, when, and how. They're fun people to be with because they are informed and adventurous. They have new information to share. They are vibrantly alive.

Isn't that the kind of people you want to raise at your house? Then encourage curiosity.

Building Values Through Curiosity

Talk About Your Discoveries

Curiosity really won't serve your purpose as a springboard for teaching values unless you talk about what you are discovering. At the bottom of the ability to communicate values lies the ability to communicate—period.

One of our favorite early spring hikes was to Boulder River Falls. By walking only two miles, you can be in a pristine wilderness where no motorized vehicles are allowed, no tree cutting takes place, and where you are surrounded by breath-taking beauty.

The path to the falls starts out wide and easy, but soon narrows to a single-file trail. On one hike we decided to stop every five minutes and talk about what we had seen. "What was the highlight of the last five minutes?" Ed would ask.

Once it was a perfect spider's web that held raindrops on each strand. Once it was a spring flower poking through the rocks. It was a tiny stream we had crossed on stones. It was a hollow log full of wood pulp and a fallen tree which had become a nurse tree for a lot of seedlings.

You don't have to be surrounded by a pristine wilderness in order to ask questions. Spiders build webs in your neighborhood as well. Just begin to be observant and curious about what you see.

Open the Door to Conversation by Asking and Allowing Questions

Here are some key questions which encourage conversation about what you are discovering:

I wonder what _____?

What if _____?

Why do you suppose _____?
Where do you think _____?
Why do you think _____?
How come _____?

Often the kids will ask questions about what they are seeing and experiencing. But if they don't, we need to be ready ourselves to open a candid conversation about the subject at hand. We aren't talking about giving them a Bible lesson. That may happen sometimes, and you should take advantage of the opportunity when it presents itself, but the point here is opening free-flowing lines of communication about topics of mutual interest. We're talking about learning to communicate about anything and everything so that later you can discuss important issues in life, like responsibility, morality, fairness and honesty, and living upright, worthwhile lives.

When a child asks point-blank questions about sex, money, divorce, remarriage, stealing, anger, relationships, and religion, it means he is ready to begin learning about these subjects. We must be ready. We cannot, because of fear or ignorance, be afraid or unwilling to discuss these important topics with him. Children instantly sense their parents' discomfort, and rather than embarrass the parent again, will stop asking questions. For example, we must overcome our own fear of death so that we can discuss with our children this experience that troubles them. Death is a part of life; just because we have isolated it from family life doesn't mean it doesn't exist. It needs to be discussed in the family setting.

We must not let our own discomfort about discussing sex keep us from open and honest communication about this subject early in the child's life. Don't you want to be the first one to discuss this important information with your child? But if you are uncomfortable talking about it with your children, they will ask their friends about sex. And while you may breathe a sigh of relief that you don't have to discuss it with them, consider the misinformation they are gathering.

When they ask you about sex and death, answer their questions. And be there for them when they are ready to discuss all other topics of importance. If we want to be the ones to influence our children's value system, we must not leave their values training to others.

When listening to a child's question, it's important that we hear not only what is said but also what isn't said. What is the body language? Is this the real issue or is something else bothering him?

At one point Mark's questioning almost drove me crazy. I think it was partially because I wasn't prepared for the level of questions he was asking.

"I'm so afraid," he would say, while he sat cluching his coat around himself.

"What are you afraid of?" we would ask.

"I'm afraid I'm not a Christian. Am I?"

"Why do you say that?" Then we would talk with him about his experience with Christ. For a while he would be all right, but soon he would return with the same statements and questions.

He was experiencing a lot of fear about this. It was affecting his eating and his sleeping. Finally we discovered that he was questioning whether God really existed. He was afraid that God would be angry with him because he had so many questions. He believed that a person who questions God is a doubter, and doubters don't go to heaven. He was terrified that he wasn't going to make it to heaven.

I know this example is a little extreme, but it gives you some idea of the kind of thoughts which can go on in a kid's head. We prayed and prayed with him, and I tried to work it through with him, but it wasn't until Ed gave him a short lesson in apologetics (a defense of the Gospel) that Mark was satisfied. Ed explained to him that it was not a sin to have questions, and that questioning is not necessarily doubting God. At last he was satisfied. It was all right to have questions. It doesn't mean you don't love God or that God is angry with you because you are unsure. Somehow it satisfied him, and it never has been a problem again.

I'm not saying that every ten-year-old child needs a course in apologetics, but I *am* saying that we need to listen not so much to the question, but to the heart's cry behind it. What is this kid needing to know by asking the question?

Parents need to take advantage of opportunities to prepare the child for life by working through the questioning with him, regardless of how long it takes. It is our responsibility and privilege to prepare him for life ahead by taking advantage of his questions and the opportunity to share our values with him.

Some parents fail at answering questions not because they don't answer the child's questions, but because they flood him with more information than he possibly can assimilate. When a child asks about sex, give him only the information he requests, instead of enough information to prepare him for marriage. In order to avoid uncomfortable or unpleasant subjects, or to hide their own ignorance, parents sometimes give their children misinformation. Misinformation stimulates fantasies and distortions in the child's mind. It's foolish to stretch the truth to our kids. They'll catch us at it eventually, and the next time we try to communicate something important, we won't be taken seriously.

We tried not to have too many rules at our house, but one firm rule was that the kids could not lie. We felt strongly about this because one lie generates another and another. The flip side of our rule was that Ed and I never told them an untruth. To this day they know that what we tell them is the truth.

I want to digress here to say that I have seen many parents set their children up to tell a lie. When you know that your child has done something wrong, don't ask him, "Did you do _____?"

If he is a normal kid, he will say no. He realizes the consequences of admitting his failures, and he would rather risk not getting caught telling a lie than suffer the consequences if he tells the truth. Now he has been backed into a corner, *and* he has lied.

It is so much better to say, "Why did you do _____?" Then he'll tell you why he did it, and you can deal with the real problem. Sometimes it is difficult for a child to tell the truth even when he knows that you know what happened. More than once we said to our children, "If you tell me the truth, you will not be punished. But if I discover you have lied to me, you will be punished for what you did, *and* you will be punished for lying." Usually they told the truth. After an explanation of why they should not have done what they did, they were released with no further punishment.

Searching for Answers

Parents don't have all the answers to life's questions, and they shouldn't pretend that they do. The search for answers to questions—starting with those resulting from your curiosity adventures to the bigger issues we have been discussing—should be a family search whenever possible. The search for answers must be open and honest.

Perhaps one of the best things a parent can do is to *not* answer the questions, but to provide the tools for finding answers—books, the Bible, or resource people. People learn best when they participate in the learning process, and are not simply fed information. We retain little of what we hear, a little more of what we see, a little more of what we both see and hear, and most of what we do.

Can you now see how using a child's natural curiosity can lead your family on one adventure after another, and how what you discover can open communication lines for the members of your family? Can you see that once the lines of communication are open, it is a short step from talking about everything in general to talking specifically about your family's values?

Today why don't you begin to stimulate your own curiosity and that of your family. Then pursue it, and see where it will take you. You might be surprised.

5

Reading: The Unlimited Adventure

We tapped on the door of a simple ranch-style house. Visiting church families around the city was one of Ed's duties as associate pastor of a growing congregation in this California town. Because we were newly married and had no children, I accompanied him on many of his visits.

The door opened, and a teenage girl smiled and invited us in. There in a big overstuffed chair sat the mother, and all around were her six children. The little ones wore their pajamas. She held the youngest child in her lap, one arm around him, and with her free hand she juggled a book.

"Oh, hello," she greeted us. "We were just reading *Huckleberry Finn.*" The children's faces showed their delight in the story they were sharing. "The children and I usually read a few evenings each week. My husband works evenings, and he can't be with us. We enjoy the stories so much," she explained.

We stayed only a few minutes. Although they were very polite, the children were anxious to continue their story. We felt that we were intruding on a very close and special moment in this family's life.

I've never forgotten that scene. At that moment I decided that when our children arrived, we would make reading a priority in our family. And we did. Over the years we read dozens of books aloud to our children.

Reading aloud together provides a forum for all kinds of discussion—first about the story, and then about the values of the people in the story, and later about your family's values on the same subject.

For example, we read the story *The Midnight Fox* with our children. In this story a young boy spends a summer on his aunt and uncle's farm. He is unhappy and bored until one day he spots a black fox in the field. That black fox absorbs his whole mind and being. It becomes the focus of his attention for the rest of the summer as he tries to hide its existence from his uncle, whose passion is hunting, and from his aunt, whose prize chickens disappear in the night, leaving behind only a pile of feathers and a telltale fox footprint in the dust.

The Midnight Fox is a wonderful story that keeps the attention of eight- to ten-year-old children, and even older. You can ask many values questions about this story: Was it right for the young boy to keep the secret of the fox from his uncle, who loved to hunt? Was it right to hide information about where the fox's den was located? Was it right not to tell his aunt that he knew about the fox even after her chickens disappeared? The story could be the launching pad for a discussion about when it is right to keep secrets and when it is not. As a parent, you can tell the child your ideas on the subject.

We cannot underestimate the importance of our personal influence upon our children and their value system. If we are able to communicate with them, we also will be able to communicate our values to them. And an excellent way to begin communicating is through reading aloud together, and talking about what you have read.

You deliberately can select a book which addresses a value you want to emphasize to your family. For example, books which address problem areas, such as lying, can be read together and then discussed. An example of positive values might be a book relating how to show kindness to disabled children. The story would open the door to discussing the needs of the disabled and what our responsibility is toward them.

Sometimes the books we read together express ideas which oppose our values—things we don't want our children to believe. Once when I was reading the children a book about the settling of New England, I was surprised to find God's name taken in vain a number of times.

The first time it happened, I stopped and looked hard at what I was seeing, because I thought I was misreading it. Of course, everyone in the family wanted to know what was wrong. So I read them what was written on the page. Whenever it came up again, I changed the text and read something else in its place.

But that's not the end of the story. I was incensed to think a children's book which took such liberty with God's name would be on a public library shelf. I asked the librarian how books were selected for the library. I then told her my complaint. Then I wrote letters expressing my displeasure to the proper officials, and I let my kids know what I was doing. In this way, we made a negative experience work to teach them how we value God's name.

Several years ago while attending a writers' conference, I discovered that some families in America still read together regularly. The late Joe Bayley, well-known writer and editor for David C. Cook Publishing Company and columnist for *Eternity* magazine, related how his family had been reading together from the time their boys were young.

First they read to the boys. Later, when the boys were teenagers, each family member took turns reading to each other. Often each person had a copy of the book the family was reading. Sometimes they read in turn, and sometimes each person read a particular character's part. Joe related what a sense of sharing the family had, and how sad they often were to see a good book end.

Adela Rogers St. Johns has said that one reason for the generation gap is that fathers and mothers don't read to their children anymore. Consequently, they don't have a common vocabulary for communication. I would like to add that the ability to communicate is essential in sharing values.

In Gladys Hunt's book about reading to children, *Honey for a Child's Heart,* she says, "If families don't read books together, how do they know each other's friends?"

If families do read books together, they will know each other's friends. They also will share special words and ideas gleaned from books. In her book *A Wrinkle in Time,* Madeleine L'Engle introduces the idea of tesseracting, in which two points in time may seem to be side by side, but actually a loop of time separates them, hence the wrinkle in time. Many times since we read that story, our family has mentioned tesseracting when we see someone we have not seen for a long time, yet it seems as if we saw them only yesterday. We realize that we have experienced a wrinkle in time.

Growing Early Readers

Several years ago our government spent much money studying how to promote early reading in children. After months and months of extensive investigation, the results were announced. The study determined that those children who learn to read early have not been taught an early-reading course, they have not been pushed to learn to read, and they have not attended expensive preschools with early-learning programs.

The survey concluded that the best way to encourage early reading is to hold a child on your lap when he is very young, and read to him. The study reported that the combination of the warmth of your arms around him and the sound of your voice, even though he may not understand the words yet, communicate to him that reading is good and books are fun, and he soon will want to learn how to read.

Joel and Cynthia Shigo are parents who believe reading is a family affair. They started reading to their girls, Catherine, who is four, and Elisabeth, who is six, as soon as they could sit up—about six months old.

Each week the girls are taken to the library, where each is allowed to choose three books. Then Cynthia picks two more for each of them. One of her two selections is usually a cookbook. During the week she lets them cook something from the cookbook. Sometimes Dad takes them to the library. When he goes with them, they usually come home with silly books.

Dad spends time alone with the girls reading to them, and Mom also reads to them independently. But they also read together as a family. They always are working on a family book project. Together they have read *The Wizard of Oz*, the Madeleine L'Engle trilogy, the Narnia series, *Heidi*, and the *Little House on the Prairie* series.

These children's teachers report that the children can tell a story. They have gained an ability to communicate, they read with expression, they have high reading skills, and they have the ability to describe something with sharp, original images. They also can make up stories, and their teachers feel they have an improved sense of humor.

A child who is familiar with books has a head start on life. From books it is possible to learn about places you never may go, and become familiar with people you never will meet. It is possible to step backward through time and understand the peoples of past centuries. From books you can learn to make houses and gardens. You can learn to repair a car, design a garment, or teach a dog to obey. You can learn about the mysteries of space and the complex world of the cell. There is a book for every idea which enters your head. And it is through a particular book, the Bible, that you and your child will learn the path to eternal life.

Where to Get Books

It takes only a little encouragement to interest a child in books. One way to expose children to books is to take them at a very early age to the library.

Some parents act as if libraries have quarantine signs on them. It's okay to take children inside. They will not catch some horrible disease there. You can begin taking children to the library as soon as they can walk. They quickly learn that their loud talking disturbs people who are there to read. They also learn where to find their favorite books. And they quickly learn that they will not be allowed to pull all the books onto the floor. Most of them try that stunt once or twice. After only one or two sessions in the library, the children will disappear to their own section and will stay there happily until the parent is ready to leave.

Most libraries have a children's corner with tables and chairs just their size. Books are arranged on low shelves, in baskets, or in display racks on the tables.

In preparing to write this chapter, I went to the library to browse around and see what was happening in the children's section. There at a blue fish-shaped table sat a little dark-haired girl, and she was reading. Periodically she walked to the bookshelf, selected another book, and then returned to her place. She was perfectly content to read while her mother searched the bookshelves in another part of the library.

My trip to the library also alarmed me. My visit was pre-Halloween, and it seemed that the library had displayed in the children's section every scary, occultish, ghoulish book that could be found.

Parents of young children tell me that public libraries have a proliferation of occult-oriented books. I believe that no one, especially children, should be reading books associated with the occult. We are warned in Scripture to stay far away from all forms of the black arts.

Because so many of these kinds of books are available now, and they are readily accessible in public libraries, parents must monitor their children's book selections until children are old enough and wise enough to leave these books alone.

Another source of books for children is the Christian bookstore. Christian publishers are busy preparing all kinds of materials for children.

One store owner excitedly told me about a new display area to be installed in her store. This display categorizes books by children's ages, and it is just the right height for children. It will take up a major part of her store.

Take your children to your local Christian bookstore, and see what is available now that might not have been there even a year or two ago.

Buy books for your children. They need to have books that are their very own. It is important that they learn how to care for their books—to respect them as friends. In learning how to care for their own books, they also will learn how to care for books which belong to others.

Another way to provide your children with their own books is to give grandparents a list of special books from which they can make selections for birthdays and Christmas. The grandparents will be thankful for the suggestions, the children will be pleased, and you will not have to return something that doesn't fit.

Secondhand stores and garage sales are good sources of used books for children. Some children want to keep their books forever. (We have some very old books on our shelves.) But most kids eventually part with their books, and they wind up

on thrift shop shelves, where you will find them for only
pennies. Kids don't care a bit if someone else has owned the
book before them. Always keep a list of books with you, and
watch for specific titles when poking around secondhand
shops.

Finding Time for Family Reading

How do you find the time to read together as a family? You
don't! You *make time* for reading. First you must ask yourself,
"Do I think it is important for our family to spend time reading
together aloud?" If the answer is yes, then you set aside time
for it. Reading together as a family never will happen unless
someone in your family is convinced that it is important.

I mentioned earlier that our family used the time driving to
and from church as a reading time. It wasn't much time—only
twenty minutes each way, but multiply that by two or three
trips in a week, and now you have two hours a week for
reading in the car.

Of course, some of these trips were made in the dark when
reading was impossible. Sometimes we preferred singing or
talking to reading. We did, however, read all the way through
Little Pilgrim's Progress and a number of other books during
those rides.

Longer driving trips provided more time for reading. In our
family, reading made getting there half the fun. I remember
reading James Herriot's stories about his life as a country
veterinarian in England. He had some of the most outrageous
experiences with animals. I remember having to stop reading
because I was laughing until the tears ran down my face and
my sides ached.

Here are some other ideas for finding time for family reading:

1. Keep a book handy for those times when you must wait for
   others. Kids hate waiting and can become unbearable. A
   good story helps to speed the time for all of you.
2. Read to your children for ten or fifteen minutes just before
   their bedtime. Reading has a tremendously soothing effect.
   Watch out for the little rascals who beg for "just one more
   story."

3. Set aside a special time each week for reading together as a family. Sunday afternoons? Saturday evenings?
4. Vacation times can be a time of reading something very special. Perhaps you'll find as we did that reading one book together generated the desire to read another. We saved some of those books for vacations when we could spend an extended time reading.
5. Remember that having a book with you, ready to be read, is better than many shelves of books unread at home.

What Shall We Read Together?

It isn't always easy to find books that appeal to all the age levels represented in a family. Some stories are enthralling to children, but become a real drag to the adults trying to wade through them.

One book we read in this category was *Charlie and the Great Glass Elevator*. Some of the Dr. Seuss books were all right the first fifty times I read them, but I must confess that they lost some of their shine after that.

But when our family walked beside a young Labrador retriever, an old English bull terrier, and a Siamese cat as they ventured across the Canadian wilderness in a book called *The Incredible Journey*, no one's attention dwindled for a moment. And when at last Bodger, the old terrier, threw himself into the waiting arms of his young master, there wasn't a dry eye in the family.

If you stumble onto a book which is either too difficult for the younger members of the family or too inane for the adults, put it aside and choose something more to the tastes of everyone. We discovered that the stories did not necessarily have to be tailored to the youngest member of the family. Although the youngest in our family may not have understood every word of what was being said, he was able to catch the gist of it, and amazingly enough, some of those big words soon crept into his vocabulary.

I remember, too, that when we began reading books without pictures, Mark grabbed my arm and pulled it so that he could look at the book. "Where's the pictures, Mom?" he asked.

"There aren't any," I told him. "You have to make the pictures in your head."

That idea was brand new to him. He accepted it, and settled down to listen. As I watched him listening, I often wondered what fantastic pictures were passing through that little mind.

What kinds of books should Christian families be reading? Should their reading be confined largely to Bible stories, missionary narratives, and biographies of Christian saints? Well, that's a good place to begin. All of these subjects are well worth the time invested in reading them. As they grow in their faith, your children will draw from these sources as examples of faithfulness and encouragement for their Christian lives.

Stories of Christian heroes such as David Livingstone, the greatest missionary explorer of them all, William Carey, the shoemaker who turned all of India upside down with the Gospel, and Mary Slessor, who poured out her life deep in the heart of Africa, will give your children food for thought and will weigh heavily on their minds as they grow. Some children will begin to contemplate, "Could it be that I could change a nation for God? Could God possibly have a plan and purpose for my life? Could God use me?"

Every family needs a good Bible storybook. Dozens of them are on the market. There is something quieting and comforting about reading Bible stories with your children. There is comfort to the child who learns that God is always there, watching over him, protecting him, and loving him. There is assurance to the parent who learns that God is pro-family, able to deliver, God over all, and in control of all things. Families who read Bible stories together will grow in their inner beings.

Mark, like many school-age children, had problems with fear, and especially at night. One night while he and I were reading together, I read this phrase which brought peace to him and great encouragement to me: "God did this for you because you trusted Him. For the eyes of the Lord are looking everywhere around the world to find those who love Him, so that He can help them" (Ken Taylor's *Living Bible Story Book*).

Somehow it sank into his head. God would be there to help

a little boy who is frightened in the night, and God would be there to help a mommy who sometimes didn't know how to cope with fear in her little boy.

Good reading for Christian families includes Bible stories and stories about Christian saints, but what else? Should Christians read fantasy? If so, what kind of fantasy? Is there any value in it?

I think there is great value in reading fantasy to children. Children seem to have the ability to take fantasy in their own stride. Certainly they get gigantic doses of fantasy on television. In fact, isn't almost everything they see on television fantasy? Yet even from fantastic, imaginary adventures, children are learning concepts of right and wrong, and of good and evil. They learn facts, cultures, language styles, and how to follow the thread of a complex narrative. Fantasy can be tremendously mind expanding, causing the readers and the listeners to think more broadly and more creatively than they have in the past.

Some of the great classics of children's literature fall into the realm of fantasy. C. S. Lewis's *Chronicles of Narnia* series, J. R. R. Tolkien's *The Lord of the Rings,* and George MacDonald's writings all are fantasy. So are *Alice in Wonderland, Gulliver's Travels,* and many others.

Family reading should encompass a broad spectrum of literature. It should include history (told at a child's level), adventure stories, poetry, biographies, humorous pieces, and animal stories. There should be picture books, including pop-up books. There should be rhyming books, books that play with words, easy-reader books, and books whose authors paint glowing landscapes with words.

Selecting the Best Books First

Every public library contains thousands of children's books. Where do you begin? Every library also has a reference section which includes books to guide parents in selecting literature for their children. Believe it or not, one of the books in that section is entitled *Exciting, Funny, Scary, Short, Different, and Sad Books Kids Like About Animals, Science, Sports, Families, Songs, and Other Things.*

There is also an "02" section where you can find similar books about children's literature. These books can be checked out and taken home to peruse at leisure. Look there for Betsy Hearne's book called *Choosing Books for Children*, which addresses the whole issue of children's literature. Jim Trelease's *The Read-Aloud Handbook* thoroughly discusses many of the subjects we have touched on in this chapter. This book also includes a treasury of read-aloud books, including the title and author, the age level for which the book was intended, and a short description of the book.

There are many other useful reference books, but my favorite is *Honey for a Child's Heart* by Gladys Hunt. In researching for this chapter, I picked up this volume again after many years, and realized I have been deeply influenced by it. She, too, discusses the pleasure of reading together as a family. And she shares her thesis that parents who read widely together with their children are those who most influence their children. It is they who will affect their children's values for good.

In the back of her book, Gladys Hunt lists the children's books she recommends, with a short description of each. Because the author is a Christian, hers may be the most trustworthy list. At any rate, she will provide you with more titles than you can read in the years you will have with your children. Her list is divided into age levels. This is the list from which our family read. And as I look through it again I recognize many old friends, and I see many books we didn't have the time to read. I'm sorry about that.

In addition to these book lists, dozens of fine new children's books are published each year, and must be evaluated by you. Because of the influence of eastern religions, New Age, and the occult, even on children's books, it is wise to pay careful attention to these books. Read new, unknown titles before your children do if you have any doubts about their content, and read them with your children whenever possible. Always be on the lookout for subtle attempts to influence the minds of children toward these philosophies.

To me, reading is and always has been the unlimited adventure. There is no room, sickbed, situation, or circumstance that can confine the mind that reads. Reading is one way to give your child wings, to push his horizons out beyond the quasars, and to free him to expand beyond his and your wildest dreams. Reading together as a family lets all of you share in that adventure, and at the same time, draw together as you learn each other's language and friends.

Below is a small sample of quality children's literature which you can read to your children. Check your public library and local Christian bookstores for more titles.

Happy reading—together!

Suggested Reading

Books to Share With Your Children:

Burnford, Sheila. *The Incredible Journey*. Boston: Little, Brown and Co., 1961. Paperback: Bantam.

Byars, Betsy. *The Midnight Fox*. New York: Viking, 1968; Penguin, 1981.

Carroll, Lewis. *Alice in Wonderland*. Illustrated by John Tenniel. Many editions. Copyright 1865.

Dahl, Roald. *Charlie and the Great Glass Elevator*. New York: Knopf, 1972.

L'Engle, Madeleine. *A Wrinkle in Time*. New York: Farrar, Straus and Giroux, 1962. Paperback: Dell.

Lewis, C. S. *The Lion, the Witch and the Wardrobe*. New York: Macmillan Publishing Co., 1950. Paperback: Macmillan.

Milne, A. A. *Winnie the Pooh*. New York: E. P. Dutton, 1962. Paperback: Dell.

Taylor, Helen L. *Little Pilgrim's Progress*. Chicago: Moody Press, n.d.

Tolkien, J. R. R. *The Lord of the Rings*. New York: Houghton Mifflin Co., 1984.

Books for You to Read More About Children's Literature:

Carroll, Frances Laverne, and Mary Meacham. *Exciting, Funny, Scary, Short, Different, and Sad Books Kids Like About Animals, Science, Sports, Families, Songs, and Other Things*. Chicago: American Library Association, 1984.

Hearne, Betsy. *Choosing Books for Children*. New York: Dell
    Publishing, 1981.
Hunt, Gladys. *Honey for a Child's Heart*. Grand Rapids: Zonder-
    van Publishing House, 1978.
Trelease, Jim. *The Read-Aloud Handbook*. New York: Penguin
    Books, 1985.

6

A Treasure in Your Own Home

A friend recently told me that his son, a builder and architect, is building a wonderful new house for himself. A focal point of this new house will be a media-entertainment room with tiered seats, wide-screen TV, slide projector, VCR, and a compact disc player.

What I find so interesting is that he is following a new trend toward making the home a center of entertainment. Demographer David Poltrack has been quoted as follows: "An evening at the Joneses' will be rated not by the quality of dinner served, but by the quality of entertainment provided. In short, evenings will not be planned, but produced."*

The home once again is gaining importance as a center of family life. If we can capitalize on this trend and make what happens in our home a time of gathering around shared experiences, we will profit. But if we simply let our machines entertain us, and we sit staring at a screen, failing to relate to our families, we will be the losers.

It is not enough to hope that family life will happen. We must rethink the way in which it happens. We need to remember that for all the outside influences in a child's life, the home still has the greatest influence. The child spends more time in the home than he does in school, at church, or in any of the other activities with which we fill our lives. Mom and Dad still have

*Daniel Poltrack in *Notes From American Demographers' Eighth Annual Demographic Outlook Conference*, June 1, 2, 1988, New York, NY.

the greatest influence on him in the early years of life. It is up to us to find a way to maximize that influence.

Family Night—A Weekly Treasure

"Hit it!"

"I got it."

"You missed."

"Okay, whose turn is it to serve?"

It was family night at our house, and we were playing balloon volleyball in the living room. We, the players, were seated on sofas and chairs facing each other. The rule was that we had to stay seated as we batted the balloon back and forth. It was fun, it was easy on the furniture, and the direction the balloon would go when batted was unpredictable, which made participants want to stand up and swat it. But if that happened, their team lost a point.

Balloon volleyball was only one of dozens of family night activities in our home. Because Ed was a busy pastor in a large church and was working up to sixty hours a week, we decided to set aside one night a week as a family night. From the start we decided this idea was not going to work unless we all committed to the idea and to each other. And when we decided that, we taught an important value—that of commitment and loyalty.

Family night is one of the ways to maximize the influence of parents and home on children. It's not a new idea. In fact, family night has been around for a number of years. But even though it is not new, it's an important idea—perhaps more important now than ever before because of our increasingly busy life-style.

What can a family do that everyone will enjoy? How do you get beyond the complaints that "this is boring"? The possibilities are limitless.

But first, you'll need some rules. I'll tell you what we did, and then you can make your own rules for your family. Let the kids make the rules; they'll be more likely to keep them if they do. You will have to keep referring to them, probably as long as you have a family night at your house. You also may have to revise them from time to time.

Here's the Weisings' set of family night rules:

1. We will keep one night a week for family. This need not be the same night every week. We'll try to plan far enough ahead so that everyone can clear his calendar and be there.
2. Each family member will take turns planning the programs for the evening. No one gets out of taking his or her turn. If one family member is very busy that week, he can switch with another family member, but he still has to take his turn later.
3. No complaining or fidgeting. No statements like, "This is dumb," or "I could have done this better." Remember, you'll get your chance to prove how good you are as we take turns planning family night events.
4. Everyone will participate and cooperate, even when the planning is done by the youngest member of the family, and may seem too elementary to the oldest. We all will participate and cooperate. (It's Mom and Dad's job to protect the self-esteem of the younger children in the home. Permanent damage can be done to fragile egos when older children are allowed to belittle younger ones in a family.)

In this first rule-setting, planning time, it also is important to talk about the purpose of family night. Communicate to each other why a family needs to get together on a regular basis. This is a great time to talk about the value of family loyalty, sharing, commitment, and togetherness.

Two purposes I would like to suggest are:

1. *To have fun together as a family.* Family night should be the most looked-forward-to night of the week. It should carry a sense of surprise and adventure. It can and should be a time of great anticipation.
2. *To worship the Lord together.* For Christian parents, a prime purpose for family night is to mold your children into strong, committed Christians, able to stand in an increasingly secular society. Family night is a time when children

can watch their parents model devotion and worship to God.

Planning Family Night

In an earlier chapter, I said you would need to take out a calendar and mark out a night each week for family night. Now is the time to mark the calendar. Decide as far ahead as possible which night will be family night each week. Scheduling the same night every week will simplify your life. We couldn't do that, and so used a different night each week.

As far ahead as possible, plan who will be in charge on a particular night. Post a schedule, and someone will have to help the younger ones remember their night. They will be learning the value of accepting responsibility and following through on an assignment.

Assign a night to each family member. That person can plan anything he wants. He will have to decide whether he can handle it alone, or if he needs Dad to drive the car somewhere, or Mom to purchase some special supplies for the event. The more the child can do on his own, the more he will learn about planning and carrying out a plan.

He should include a related Scripture and a prayer time in his family night plan. Once again, younger children may need some help, but let them go as far as they can on their own. What they need most is encouragement. The Scripture can be from a favorite storybook or from an easy-to-read Bible. The prayer can be one or two sentences from each member of the family. God isn't concerned about complexity or finesse of the prayer and Bible reading, and we shouldn't be either.

Suggested Family-Time Events

Here are some ideas to get you started thinking about your family night:

CONCERN NIGHT Plan a family project to help someone like a missionary, elderly person, shut-in, relative, or someone who needs encouragement.

I remember the fun we had putting together a survival kit for a young woman who moved from Seattle to my small hometown in Montana. This was an unheard of event. People leave that little town in droves to seek their fame and fortune in the big cities around the country. No one ever *moves* from a big city to that mountain village.

My children often had visited their grandparents, who still live there. They knew what it would be like for this young woman to exchange neon marquees for two stoplights hanging in the middle of Main Street. They knew that rapid transit there often means a four-wheel rig, not a high-speed train.

I don't remember all the things that went into that survival kit, but I do remember that the children insisted on including mosquito repellent and insect bite medicine. They too often had been victims of the whining, blood-sucking hordes of mosquitoes which drive man and beast to distraction during the early summer in Montana.

We probably included a book or two for the long, slow evenings. There may have been fishhooks since the town's common philosophy is that "God doesn't take away from a man's life the hours he spends fishing."

We plotted, planned, laughed, and laughed some more as we packed the box. I remember the children ran all over the house gathering things to tuck into the box. It was a lot of fun.

CELEBRATION NIGHT   Plan a party to honor someone in the family on a special occasion (like a good report card) or plan a party to celebrate some special day (like St. Patrick's Day). We'll give you more ideas about celebrating in a later chapter.

FUN NIGHT   Plan an evening of fun and games at home. I have to confess that I hate table games, and whenever possible, I squirm my way out of them. Whenever table games were the main event of the evening, I had to check my attitude. I usually tried to make popcorn or a dessert while the games were being played. But when I did sit down and play with the entire family, it almost caused a celebration.

OUTING NIGHT   Plan some kind of adventure away from home. Earlier I told you about our trip to the observatory. That was an outing night. On another outing night we went to the circus. (Ed asked me what I wanted for my birthday, and I told him I wanted to take the kids to the circus. It was probably the best birthday present I ever had.)

On another outing night we took advantage of a very special Christmas event in our area. All of the boat owners decorate their boats with lights and play Christmas music. Everyone on board ship dresses in Christmas costumes, and then they parade their boats from one lake to another through a body of water known as the Montlake Cut.

For years a family in our church has lived on a houseboat floating in the Montlake Cut. One year they invited us to their home to watch the Christmas ships. We bundled up in coats and scarves, stood on their houseboat deck, drank hot cider, and watched the ships sail by. It was a very special evening.

MEDIA NIGHT   Plan and give a media presentation using slides, filmstrips, homemade videos, cartoon strips, and other visual aids.

Wendy spent weeks producing a wonderful slide presentation. I took shots of Mark and Wendy together. Then Wendy raided my slides for others she wanted to use. She organized the slides to coordinate with a popular song about believers falling into the arms of God the Father. Then she gathered all the pictures she could find of both her father and grandfather holding children in their arms. When we viewed it together—over and over—there wasn't a dry eye in the place. We forgot about putting the slides back in order, and for months we replayed that slide presentation.

PROJECT NIGHT   Provide materials for the family to make a project—art, drama, making a game, handicrafts, or something else.

At our house the project often was a puppet show. We accumulated an impressive selection of puppets over the years. Some were gifts from relatives, some I found in thrift shops, and some I made. Some of our favorites were puppets made from paper bags or socks. It wasn't the artistic quality of the puppets that mattered, but the fun of making and using them.

Sometimes a Bible story looked quite strange when Daniel was played by a dog puppet and Esther by a sock puppet, but where the visual image failed, the kids' imaginations soared. It just didn't matter how true to life the puppets were.

A puppet theater need be no more than a large cardboard

box with a hole cut in it, set on a table, or you can forget the box and let the puppeteers operate from behind the sofa.

Drama was another fun event at our house, and we all got involved. I usually pulled the shades so we didn't have to explain to the neighbors why we were running around in our bathrobes and wearing crowns on our heads.

I have a huge, old-fashioned trunk that to this day is stuffed with costumes. It is the accumulation of years of spontaneous drama. It is not as stuffed as it once was, because recently we hauled a big suitcase of costumes across the Atlantic to Wendy. I was a little concerned that a customs agent might open one of those suitcases, and we'd have to explain the presence of the red yarn, Raggedy Ann wig, a doctor's coat, and a polyester plaid jacket so loud it made your eyes hurt. However, we didn't get stopped, and we didn't have to explain.

We kept accumulating costume pieces until, by the time the children were grown, they could assemble costumes for just about any dramatic event imaginable. Both of the kids became very proficient at spontaneous drama—drama which often has me howling in side-splitting laughter. They, along with some of their friends, are in great demand as entertainers for banquets, missions programs, and youth events. And it all began in our living room.

During our family dramas we would read a Bible story together, and then decide how to dramatize it. Each family member chose or was assigned a part. Then he dug into the costume trunk for something appropriate to wear. We would act out the story, sometimes switching parts several times during the evening. Usually the kids wanted to do "just one more" drama.

OUTREACH NIGHT   Discuss and plan with the family a way to influence some other family for Christ. This might be the most difficult family night event of all. One way to influence another family for Christ is to pray for them. That isn't too difficult. It is a little harder to reach out to those people in some way. Yet, as Christians, our purpose and calling on earth is to reach the lost. We must continue to emphasize this value on an ongoing basis to our children.

One time we read the Great Commission (Matthew 28:18–

20). We formed a prayer list for other families, and then we discussed ways we could reach those people for Christ. We decided we could invite them to a special event at our church, ask them to our home for dinner, share something we have, or take them something—like a cake or a meal. As we did these things, we would look for an opportunity to share Christ with them.

We still are praying for some of those people who have not yet found the Lord, but some of the people we prayed for have become Christians. Most notable was a family of boys who lived a couple of houses away and spent their summers lobbing eggs onto our house and into our backyard. After a while the entire family found Christ, and their conversion brought peace to the neighborhood.

Our own children have been influenced profoundly by the emphasis on reaching the lost. Wendy plans to spend her life in Europe telling people about Christ. Mark hopes to be involved in international business and combine business with some kind of missions work. They are very aware that a lost world—right outside the comfortable confines of our homes—must be reached for Christ.

BIBLE NIGHT   Find a Scripture passage which is meaningful to the person in charge of family night, and provide a fun way to discuss it together, or make it come alive through many of the avenues we have discussed—drama, media, project, and so on.

A fun exercise is to read a Bible passage, and then give magazines to family members. Let them tear out and glue onto a poster—collage fashion—pictures that illustrate the meaning of the Bible passage.

TALK-IT-OVER NIGHT   Select a topic and write discussion questions. Then sit and talk about it. This activity helps to develop your children into good conversationalists—people who can think for themselves, and who can express their ideas well. Some children are more verbal than others, so watch that one or two don't dominate the conversation.

It is possible in a talk-it-over night to approach important subjects before they become problem areas. It is much better to say, "What would you do if your best friend offered you drugs?" or "If some really popular kids wanted you to cut school and hang out at the mall all afternoon, what would you do?" than to later wish you had discussed it.

Some other possible general topics are: how to find God's will for your life, how to deal with temptation, what to do when someone swears at you or takes God's name in vain, how to react when someone calls you a "Sunday school boy," or how to have personal devotions.

MUSIC NIGHT Plan a singing time with old and new songs. Musical innovations might include an "anything band" consisting of pots, pans, waxed paper on a comb, kazoos, harmonicas, and boxes to pound on like drums; tape recordings of your family singing together; puppets singing; favorite records; or Christian groups on video (you can rent from a local Christian bookstore).

It doesn't matter whether the result is more noise than music. The important thing is the involvement of the whole family singing. The music can be secular or religious, old or new, action choruses or classical music, or it can be a recital by a family member who is learning to play an instrument.

READING NIGHT We've spent an entire chapter talking about the importance of reading together as a family. Here I will just say that it is a good idea to spend an occasional family night reading together.

SHOW-AND-TELL NIGHT Each family member shares something—a hobby, collection, object, an interesting incident, something he has seen or read, or even a favorite riddle or joke. Let each person share several things.

One show-and-tell night when Wendy was in junior high and Mark was about eight, I brought out the satin slippers both of them had worn home from the hospital when they were newborns. We laughed as they now tried to squeeze the tiny shoes over their big toes. In that moment Ed and I realized how quickly they had grown up and how little time we had left with them. It was a funny, poignant moment.

SURPRISE NIGHT Plan something that will be a complete surprise to the family, such as inviting a special guest to visit, showing photographs which the family has not yet seen, going on a treasure hunt, eating something delicious together, playing a new game, or going out to some new place.

At our house surprise night was always the favorite family night. Kids love to be surprised and to plan surprises for others. Sometimes our surprise was something as simple as going to a local shopping mall and then visiting an ice cream parlor. It doesn't have to be fancy; it just has to be unexpected and unknown to the participants.

FAMILY COUNCIL   Last, but certainly not least, is family council—a time for airing things. Plan topics that the entire family can discuss. These can be problem areas that need to be dealt with or constructive suggestions about how to improve family life. Topics could include behavior in church, things I wish you wouldn't do, finances, family chores, and vacation plans.

The secret to a successful family council is open sharing, and that includes Mom and Dad as well. Many times our children confronted us about embarrassing things we had said to their friends, about talking to them like they were babies, and about not letting them finish what they had to say before making a judgment call.

Ed and I had to learn to take criticism from them and admit our guilt when necessary. Likewise, the children had to learn to take criticism and admit their guilt when we discussed their attitude problems, sloppiness in their rooms, not finishing chores, or laxness about homework.

It was easier for them to admit their error when Mom and Dad were willing to do so. During our family councils we also discussed positive subjects with the children. We told them about financial goals we were trying to accomplish and how we stood on those projects. We laid plans for vacations and mini-trips, and invited their input. We shared goals and dreams. In short, this was a family business meeting in which everyone had an equal voice and an equal vote. Although we had regularly scheduled times for family council, anyone in the family could call a spur-of-the-moment session whenever one was needed to discuss a pressing problem.

I'm sure that one of the reasons for the smoothness of our family life was this family council where we aired our differences and shared our dreams. People who share—care. We cared for each other, and the sharing helped us understand how the others were feeling.

Using TV to Instill Values

With all the negative talk about television, this section's title might startle you. Can TV really be used to instill values? Yes, I think it can, *but* it takes some serious consideration.

The major problem with television from a shared experience standpoint is that it isn't shared. TV has become our entertainment, our baby-sitter, our company. In some homes the TV is always on, regardless of what's on and whether anyone actually is watching it. It just keeps up its incessant din in the background.

If television is to become a shared family experience, then everyone in the family must sit down together and view the programs. Right there we create an interesting problem. The family first must agree about what program to watch. Communication, compromise, and cooperation come into play almost instantly when the family begins to discuss what to watch.

The other problem with television is that it is an observer activity, not a participatory one. Did you ever notice that people on TV usually are not sitting around watching TV? How boring that would be—to watch people watching TV. We like to watch TV because the characters are interacting. The more action, the better we like it.

In order for TV to be a shared experience with some interaction between family members, you must find a way to make it participatory. One way is to talk about what you are seeing. Rather than watching the screen until your eyeballs are fried, how about watching one program and then turning it off and talking about what you have viewed?

There are some fine, family-oriented programs on TV today—programs which portray your values. But sometimes programs which have been okay all year will run something that will make your hair stand on end. Sometimes it involves the occult, the New Age, or a different set of moral values than your family espouses.

Because you have grown to trust the program, you aren't expecting this problem. Suddenly, there it is. It is important to say to your kids right then, "You know, the Bible has something to say about this" or "Those are the values of the person who wrote the script, but our family believes . . ." or "In our family we don't do that." Then you'll have to decide whether it is bad enough to turn off the TV at that moment, or whether it is all right to watch until the end of the program and then talk about it.

Watch for subtle put-downs of fathers, parents, and women. Watch for the sexually suggestive, and talk about it right then. Watch for derogatory words like *nerd*, *dumbo*, and *idiot*. Point out the differences between what's being portrayed and your own stand on important issues.

At the same time, applaud television that stands up for moral values. There are some excellent series which consistently tackle problem areas for young people such as drugs, smoking, stealing, and premarital sex.

Wisdom says that we must control TV; we can't let it control us. Invest weekly in a *TV Guide*, and look through it as soon as you get it. Before viewing time choose the programming appropriate for your family. In other words, don't just watch everything that comes on, but select what you are going to see.

Over the years TV has become increasingly immoral, increasingly blatant, and more insulting to our intelligence. How much of that is enough for your family? Each family needs to decide about TV and its use in the home. But please, do decide to take some kind of action regarding TV. Decide to take control of it; don't let it control you. Use it wisely and well. Make it a shared experience, especially with younger children.

Ask yourself these questions to discover whether you are controlling TV or it's controlling you:

1. Are household members watching TV rather than doing assigned tasks—such as homework or chores?
2. Would the family rather stay home and watch television than go to church?
3. Do family activities seem boring? Would members rather watch television than participate in a family activity?

4. Have TV personalities and characters, even fictional ones, become a main topic of family conversation?
5. Is there conflict over which program to watch?
6. Does something which would have shocked you once no longer shock you?
7. Has TV become a baby-sitter?
8. Would people rather stay up and watch late-night TV than go to bed at a reasonable time?

It is important to know where the OFF switch is on our television sets and to use it, even amidst howls of protest. If you can't control TV, you might consider storing it in a closet and bringing it out only for special programs. We have found that when our television viewing is controlled and carefully selected, we enjoy the little we see ten times more than we would if we watched everything. Try it. After a few days of withdrawal, you might even like it.

At our house we tried—and sometimes failed—to control TV viewing. One of our children is very visually oriented. That doesn't just mean TV, but drama, films, anything you view. I think it comes close to an addiction for that child. The other one can take TV or leave it. People are different and respond differently to TV.

As children grow older, there comes a time for the parents to let go in lots of areas, and TV is one. Now is the time to see if what you taught them will stick. Give them time. Remember it sometimes takes a while for them to find their own way. The chances they will make right choices are increased if you have watched television with them and if they have a strong set of values.

Dinner Time—A Special Treasure

Dinner can be one of the best times for the family to share and communicate on a daily basis. However, I suspect that the American family's dinner time is almost nonexistent in many cases. I imagine that the kids grab something on their way to a sports activity, and Dad reaches home long after other family members have left for the evening's activities.

I heard about a family who sold their dining room table because no one used it anymore. All of their eating was done from trays in front of the TV. The mother in the family cooked a big pot of something and left it on the stove. Whenever anyone was hungry, he dished up something and sat down in front of the TV to eat it.

What a loss! What a tragedy to lose this special time when family members can touch base and share what has happened throughout the day. What a shame to lose one of the times when kind gestures can be done for other members of the family—gestures such as special foods, pretty dishes, flowers, and maybe even candlelight!

It takes such little effort to make dinner special: cloth or even lovely paper napkins, beautiful but inexpensive glassware, practical but lovely flatware and dishes, or a candle. A candle costs but a few pennies and adds such a festive air. Inexpensive flowers are available at the grocery store. Even a simple bowl of fruit looks pretty and helps lend an elegant air to the table.

Food can be special, too, because even if Mom works, there are wonderful dishes that can be prepared in minutes. Almost any food anyone could want now comes ready to eat in a few minutes. Even if you start with fresh vegetables and other food, many homes have microwaves which cook food quickly. There really is no excuse for sloppy, uninteresting, unappealing food preparation. Here is an area where one can say, "I care" with such little effort.

And Mom doesn't have to do all the cooking either. Even small children can and should be taught to help. They can learn how to set a pretty table. Everyone needs to pitch in and help, especially if everyone in the family works or goes to school.

After the meal is prepared, the table set, and all have been seated around the table, then what? I heard about two families, each of which did something unique. In one, the father asked the children each evening what new thing they had learned that day. He expected them to have an answer for him. Just before dinner youngsters could be seen thumbing through an encyclopedia to look for something to report. In another family the father asked what new word the children had learned that day. Here the children used the dictionary every day to find a new word to share. Those families built knowledgeable, alert, observant people.

You may want to include these ideas in your family's schedule, or you might want to come up with some ideas that are unique to your family. People—including children—like to share what is happening in their world. Parents need to encourage individual feelings and independent thinking. At our tables our children should be safe to express feelings and independent thoughts.

During dinner you may hear things you may not hear at any other time. You may hear your children's friends' values being mouthed back by your children. Right then with a few simple words—maybe with some questions to help your child evaluate what he has just told you—you can realign *your* values in your child.

Mealtime should be a pleasant, happy time of sharing over God's good gifts of food, family, shelter, and peace. Try to keep it so in your home. Sometimes, because everyone is filled with the stresses of the day, mealtime is anything but peaceful and happy. Strive for peace if at all possible.

Visitors on Purpose

There is much to be gained by using your home and your table for hospitality. It is a biblical value that should be emphasized in today's busy life-style.

Our table has been the crossroads of the world on more than one occasion. I remember a couple of British heritage who stayed with us two weeks. They taught me how to make tea in the proper, British manner. I remember other meals where people from South America, Africa, and Europe all sat down together at our table at the same time.

In addition to their friendship and wonderful stories, our international guests have presented us with treasures. We have ostrich eggs from the Kalahari, an African chief's shield and spears, a soapstone figure of a Zimbabwe bird, maracas from the Caribbean, and a tiny Greek copper plate decorated in ancient motif. All of these were gifts from people who ate with us. Those items have made countless trips to school for show and tell.

Think about inviting some senior adults to your home to share with your family. Their stories of life in earlier times will stretch your children's imagination and broaden their knowledge of life in past times.

There is a wonderful older couple with whom we have been friends for most of my children's lives. Even though our two children now are grown, when they hear that we have planned dinner or an evening with this couple, they rearrange their schedules to spend part of the evening with them. These people have laughed with us, cried with us, prayed with us, and just generally cared for us. They are ageless, and besides, they play a mean game of pool. We still are hoping someone in our family can whip them. I am so glad that my kids had the opportunity to know these people.

Invite families with children the same age as your children. We used to have so much company that if we ever ate alone on a Sunday, the kids complained that we never had company. That wasn't quite true, but it indicated how much our children enjoyed guests. It's good for families to have fellowship with other families.

Invite your pastor and his family to your home. Get to know them as people. They are just like you. They laugh, they cry, they get hurt, they enjoy success, and they suffer failure. And believe it or not, they may not get asked to their parishioners' homes as often as you think they do.

Your children will have a new perspective on the man who stands in the pulpit each Sunday if they can see him up close and in their own home. They will admire him if you are consistent in what is said about him on the days when he is not in your home. Teach your children to value your church and its leaders.

Invite other kinds of interesting people to your home. Do you know an artist, a nurse, a guitar teacher, an actress, a drummer, a painter, or a foreign-born person living in your community? Bring these people into your home one at a time and let your children talk with them. If you know that the person has something he can do or show, ask him to bring it along so the kids can experience his talent.

My daughter's roommate recently played a nose flute and several other small native instruments for us. A young man we befriended was an expert at both juggling and using a yo-yo, and often entertained us at home. Some people are great storytellers. Some are rock or coin collectors. All have something with which to enrich your children's lives and light a spark in them.

If you make your home and your table a place of hospitality, your children will learn the value of hospitality, and will become hospitable people. But more than that, each guest adds to your child's life something that no one can take away.

Value people, value talent, value relationships with these people. Let your children share in their lives, and let them share in your children's lives.

Work as a Shared Experience

Not all shared experiences which take place in the home have to be recreational. There is tremendous value in teaching children how to work. Work can be fun if approached in a positive manner.

The only negative aspect about teaching children to work is that by the time they have mastered a task so that they are really helpful, they leave home.

Each spring when we were growing up, my two brothers and I did specific chores in our yard. One of my tasks was to remove chaff from the columbines so that the new growth could begin. It was a job I liked to do because soon after the old stuff was removed the new growth would begin. I liked to check back in a few days and see if they were growing. I don't remember what my brothers' tasks were, but we all worked together as a family.

Both of our children have learned how to cook the basics, and Wendy has become an excellent gourmet cook and baker. Cooking is a fun task that can be a real help to a working mother, but only if the kitchen isn't turned into a disaster area in the process. We had a simple rule: "I don't care how big a mess you make—just clean it up."

Children, and especially young people, need to learn basic clothing care such as washing and ironing. Learning these things can be a shared experience for a family. Basic cleaning and straightening are important skills everyone needs to learn.

Invest the time to teach your children some basic work skills and you quickly will gain back a worker. Children who learn the value of work are highly employable and will have little difficulty finding and keeping a job.

Although I wasn't always sure if Mark was learning to work while he was growing up, after graduating from high school, he was hired by a bank where he is now a teller and book-keeper. He expects to be moved into the bank's international division in the near future. He is a valued employee, and somewhere he learned to work.

A strong relationship exists between responsibility of any kind and self-esteem. Work is a responsibility that, when executed well, builds self-esteem. Learning responsibility isn't just "doing chores"; it is taking ownership of a task and being loyal to it. It isn't necessarily doing something perfectly; it is doing it consistently. Responsibility should be geared to a child's ability, and when it is done well it should be honored and recognized.

The other side of responsibility is that a child has to be allowed to live with the consequences of his own irresponsi-bility. If he fails to execute his task, he must be allowed to take what comes as a result of his failure. Teaching children responsibility is a long, slow process. Hang in there—it will come.

The four walls you live within are not a home. They are a house. A home is what happens among the people who live inside those four walls. A home is a place where values can be learned as children are encouraged, instructed, and nurtured. A home is a place of sharing, and probably the most important thing you can share there are your values, the fabric of which your child's life will be constructed.

7

Collecting Waterfalls
Without a Jar

"Awww! If you've seen one waterfall, you've seen them all," a friend told us one day. "Don't you get tired of looking at waterfalls?"

"Nope," we told him.

"How many waterfalls are you hoping to collect?" he asked.

"Just as many as we can reach in a lifetime."

Some people collect salt and pepper shakers, some rocks, others baseball caps, fishing lures, or who knows what. People like to collect things. We decided that our family would collect waterfalls. You don't need a jar to collect a waterfall, but you do have to work to make this collection. About the only way to collect a waterfall is to get out and hike, so that's what we decided to do. We hiked and took photos, and that's how we built our collection. (If you live in a city and never get near a waterfall, stay with me. I have some ideas for city dwellers, too.)

At first we took little half-mile to one-mile treks back into the woods. On the way we looked at foliage, flowers, rocks, trees, seedpods, and mushrooms. The woods became as familiar to us as our own backyard. If there were berries, we walked slowly while Mark ate his way along the trail. Usually we tried to wait to eat our official lunch until we reached the falls, but sometimes we stopped along the way to eat. I think we sometimes ate more than we walked.

When we arrived at the falls we'd take pictures. If it was warm the kids would play in the water, and Ed and I would sit resting and talking while enjoying the beauty around us.

Each waterfall has its own unique setting. We could get

behind some of them and look out through the water. Some waterfalls shot tons of spray into the air and gave us a fair soaking. Some had deep pools at their base, and some had shallow bubbling streams. Some of the waterfalls came down in a sheet of water, and some divided into two streams midway. Some were blue-white with glacial silt, and some fell thousands of feet to a shelf and then continued cascading down the mountain.

A really tough hike was to Comet Falls, Washington State's highest waterfall. To reach it you have to hike for almost three hours (with kids) and gain an elevation of 1900 feet in two and a half miles. You climb up and up switchbacks for about a mile, then—still climbing—you traverse a boulder-strewn meadow. At times the path squeezes between the boulders. After wading a stream, you climb one more hill, make one more turn—and there it is—350 feet of thunder pounding onto the rocks below. This is one of those spray-casting, rainbow-producing water-falls. We were so hot by the time we arrived that we stood in the spray and let it soak us.

I'll never forget the experience we shared with the kids' grandfather in Montana at a little stream that originates in a hot springs. After flowing across meadows for miles the water still is warm when it cascades over a cliff. Someone has dammed up the stream below the falls and made a wading pool. Grandpa and the kids stood in the warm water beneath the falls and took the pounding of their lives—all the while laughing and laughing.

Why so much fuss about waterfalls? It isn't the waterfalls. It isn't the hiking. It's the shared experience of being together and gathering, not waterfalls, but memories. People who hike together learn how to talk to each other. People who sit together, eating a sandwich and viewing God's magnificent handiwork, have to work very hard at carrying a grudge. The shared experience draws a family closer.

Don't let me give you the false impression that all of our day hikes began cheerfully. There were real grumps at our house on some mornings when we wanted to hike. Once in a while somebody got sick in the car on the way. Someone *always* complained about climbing hills. (After the kids left home, I learned that when you don't have kids along, you don't have an excuse to stop every fifty feet to rest. Whew!)

Usually we ignored the grumbling and packed the knapsack. Then we stuffed kids, coats, rain gear, and lunch into the car and went anyway. They almost always got over their grumpiness. Sometimes they did and I didn't. I was particularly grumpy the day it wouldn't quit raining and raining. Ed kept saying, "I think it's clearing up." But rain still was pouring out of a black sky. Rain was running down my neck inside my raincoat. Cold, miserable, unending rain.

At last I'd had it and said, rather forcefully, "I'm not having fun. I'm miserable. I want to go home! Now!" We went home.

What Can Your Family Collect?

What can your family collect without a jar? The possibilities are unending.

ROCKS   Kids like to collect rocks—pretty-colored ones, heart-shaped rocks, round, smooth rocks, and plain, gray, ugly rocks for reasons only they know.

Rockhounding, however, is a hobby that many adults enjoy. If this appeals to you and your family, find out where the local rockhounds do their collecting and what it is they are gathering. Maybe you'll want to invest in a small rock tumbler. Even plain beach pebbles become beautiful when highly polished.

One kind of rock to collect is agates. They can be found in streambeds, on ocean beaches, in fields, and in gravel banks. There are blue agates, moss agates, beautiful banded agates from the shores of Lake Superior in Minnesota, and probably lots of other kinds of agates available all over this country.

SEASHELLS   You can look for seashells on every ocean beach in the country.

GEODES   You can collect geodes in Montana, Arizona, Oregon, and many other places. We used to pick up geodes when I was a kid. It was fun to look for the small, round, pockmarked stones. Then Dad would break them open with a hammer so that we could see the crystal-filled interior.

BIRDS   You can collect birds with a camera or in your memory.

When we were at the Grand Canyon recently, we watched eight or ten western bluebirds drinking and splashing about in the drinking fountain. Bluebirds are rather a rare sight these days, unless you know where to look. We can take you to a meadow where almost every fence post bears a bluebird house and hundreds of birds are engaged in the busy activities of their lives.

On a short hike recently we watched a rather large bird swooping and diving over a small lake. We thought that it might be the rather rare osprey, a fish hawk, but we weren't sure. In fascination, we watched his airborne choreography. In a few minutes a ranger came along and confirmed that it was indeed an osprey. What a wonderful experience to share as a family.

We all treasure a time when we drove up a river where the bald eagles spend the winter. Dozens of them were in the trees and riding the wind currents. Some of them were on a sand bar devouring the fish they had caught in the river. It would be a thrill for almost anyone to see one bald eagle, the symbol of our national heritage, but to see dozens was memorable indeed.

If you can't get to the country, don't worry. Cities are full of birds. Don't despise starlings, sparrows, pigeons, crows, blackbirds, magpies, and other city-dwelling birds. Take the time as a family to learn how many of these birds came to live in this country. It is very interesting.

FLOWERS   Walk through a vacant city lot—and look small. Some of the tiny plants at your feet bear miniscule flowers with wonderful marking and coloring. We have seen some which resemble orchids. Flowers this small often are overlooked because of their size. But small children like small things, and if the whole family can sit down in a weedy, vacant lot and examine a patch of earth, you will see things you never have seen before. It may well be your child who discovers them for you.

You can visit a park, a test garden, or a farm where flowers are grown for seed. Visit a bulb farm. Walk in the woods at different times of the year and watch for flowers you never have seen.

Buy a book that identifies wild flowers. Gather blossoms, but only if the flowers are plentiful and if it's all right to do so where you are walking. Press them between paper towels in the pages of a book until they are dry. Then your family will have a visible reminder of a shared experience.

Visit orchid houses, begonia gardens, or poinsettia farms. Visit a conservatory in a park. Conservatories often house banana plants, orchids, cactuses, seasonal flowers, flowering vines, and all kinds of unusual plants. What a treat to step out of a wintry day into the tropical environment of a conservatory! For a few minutes you can pretend you are basking in the sun on a tropical island.

Visit a local nursery seasonally. In early spring one of the big nurseries in our area is filled with primroses of every color. Later there are seemingly acres of geraniums, petunias, and roses. Then come the chrysanthemums of every hue imaginable, and finally poinsettias blazing away—row upon row— red, white, and pink.

There are thousands of places and ways to collect experiences, and so much of it doesn't need to cost you one cent. But it will cost you some effort and time. In exchange, you receive wonderful memories and experiences for your family.

One of the positive aspects about collecting birds, flowers, or whatever is that you never know when you'll be able to add to your collection. It can happen unexpectedly. Once when we were driving through the fog on our way to San Francisco, Canadian geese suddenly fell from the sky and landed on every available inch of water. A huge migratory flight had been caught in the fog, and the geese were being forced down to rest and feed. It was a rare and wonderful sight, and one I always hoped I'd see repeated, but never have.

MUSEUMS You can collect museums. Almost every town and village in the country has some kind of museum, and each one has a distinctive flavor.

Native American museums are abundant throughout the country. There are industrial, air, historical, and mining museums. Some museums feature futuristic artwork and displays. Open-air museums demonstrate the life-styles of different historical periods. There are museums attached to candy factories, near schools, and in ghost towns. In some instances, whole towns are a kind of museum: Virginia City, Montana; Cripple Creek, Colorado; Deerfield Village, Michigan; and Williamsburg, Virginia.

And of course, there's the granddaddy museum of them all, the Smithsonian, which really is a collection of museums. It would not be hard to spend weeks viewing everything on display. Our children's favorite museum at the Smithsonian was the Natural History Building which has a live insect collection. Children are allowed to hold the bugs on their fingers. Some of the bugs looked like something out of a space movie, and some of them hissed and made other strange noises. Others glowed with iridescent colors. Our two kids enjoyed themselves so much that we had a hard time pulling them away from that exhibit.

If you live in southern California, the museum at Long Beach which houses Howard Hughes's Spruce Goose is worth a visit as is a stop at the museum's neighbor, The Queen Mary.

ART GALLERIES   You can collect art galleries. Many small cities have art galleries. Visit them and see what they offer—impressionistic paintings, old masters, early American primitives, or some other style. All large cities have at least one, and usually several, art galleries.

We waited until our children were school age to take them to art galleries. But what a thrill it was for them to see the original works of art that had been pictured in their school textbooks. Sometimes when they saw a painting which had been reproduced time and again on a Christmas card, they had a hard time believing they were seeing the real thing.

Some galleries will let you take pictures as long as you don't use a flash. Others strictly forbid photographs. Ask an employee about the gallery's photo policy. You may be able to gather works of art with your camera to later view and discuss as a family.

Most art museums also have shops where you can buy inexpensive postcards and reproductions of the kids' favorite paintings. Buy them. Frame them and hang them in your home as an opportunity for remembering your shared experience of visiting the gallery and for influencing your children's value of art.

The National Gallery of Art at the Smithsonian houses one of the finest collections of impressionistic paintings in the world. It also is filled with American art treasures and hundreds and hundreds of superb masterpieces from around the world. Here you can purchase fine reproductions on an excellent paper for around a dollar each.

Neighborhood Walks

Regardless of where we are traveling, our family enjoys stopping at some village or small town, getting out of the car, and walking. It's most fun if a street fair or a farmers' market is in progress. If not, we begin searching for the local bakery or specialty shops.

Once we spent a night in Rome, New York, and were enchanted by this city's Italian flavor. We were delighted to find *gelato* (Italian ice cream) shops, fresh pasta hanging in shop windows, and a *bols* (a European game played with weighted balls) tournament in progress right behind our motel. Here was a bit of the old country's traditions being remembered in America.

Most cities are made up of many neighborhoods, each with its own flavor and identity. Those neighborhoods are places to go exploring. Visit the shops, walk the streets, talk to longtime residents, and listen to the sounds of that neighborhood—streetcars, buses, trolleys, church bells, and factory whistles. Use all your senses to learn about this new area. Eat borsch in a Russian restaurant, or croissants and crepes at a French restaurant, or have high tea in an English tearoom. All of these places can be found in most cities.

ARCHITECTURE Even if you live in a small town you can experience much together as a family simply by becoming aware of your surroundings. The little town where I was born had some beautiful homes, but I hardly noticed them back then. It wasn't until I grew up, moved away, and then returned to visit that I really saw them. There was a European-style chateau and a Spanish-style house. The front of one home had an elk head mounted and displayed under glass. A two-story brick mansion just down the street had belonged to a Civil War general. We called it The Haunted House.

Several years ago we purchased a book that describes architecture in our area. It also relates the history of many of the buildings. It is great fun to walk through a neighborhood and read about the various houses or buildings on a block. Reading that book has taught us to look up beyond the remodeled storefronts. When you look up, you see all kinds of interesting things—including gargoyles, lions, and other creatures.

There is a wonderful building in Seattle that is called the Arctic Building. All around the facade, about fifteen feet high, are walrus heads. Many years ago after a severe earthquake the tusks were removed to keep them from falling to the street below. The first time our family took a city walk, that's the way we saw the walruses—tuskless. But a couple of years ago the tusks were replaced, and now all around the building benign tusked walruses peer down at gawkers.

Collect old houses for your shared experience memory book. Charitable groups often persuade owners of lovely old and unique homes to open them to the public once a year. They charge a small admission fee. Other old homes belong to the state and are open for viewing throughout the year. Most of these are furnished in period furnishings. It's fun to see the interesting tools and furnishings our recent ancestors used in their daily lives. Take pictures, keep a notebook, and see how many old houses and antique items of interest you can collect.

Getting Ready to Go

One-day outings should be relaxed, fun times of sharing experiences. A little preparation and thought can ensure they are. Here's a short checklist for day-trippers and hikers.

SHOES Forget fashion, and wear comfortable walking shoes. Blisters are no fun, so if there is the slightest possibility anyone will develop a blister, bring along Band-Aids or better still, adhesive moleskin. The minute anyone feels a hot spot, stop immediately and apply moleskin to it.

BACKPACK Even for city walkers, a backpack is a useful place to tuck all kinds of things. I used to feel like a pack animal when hiking with my family. The kids always were asking me to carry their jackets or some treasure they had discovered. We should have insisted that everyone in our family carry a backpack.

JACKETS OR SWEATERS "Always be prepared" is a good motto. Every year people die of hypothermia because they are unprepared for a sudden shift in the weather. It doesn't have to be very cold for people, especially children, to suffer hypothermia. Hypothermia occurs when the body loses heat faster than it can replace it. Hypothermia can result in extreme shaking, disorientation, and death. Getting soaked hastens the process.

A wool sweater and a raincoat, or even a large plastic bag which can be worn as a raincoat, tucked into the backpack is good insurance against hypothermia. Even when wet, wool helps the body retain heat.

FOOD Little people (and big people too) don't have much fun if they are hungry. Carry snacks and dispense them lavishly. I used to make something called "gorp," a combination of nuts, raisins, chocolate chips, coconut, and anything else that can be scooped up and eaten from the hand. Fruit is heavy to carry, but makes a good snack. Granola bars and dried fruit are also good snacks.

Take drinking water along if you won't be able to purchase drinks. Never drink from streams and rivers. Even in the remotest places, they are polluted because there are so many hikers. Drinking polluted water can make you extremely ill.

CAMERA If you're going to collect without a jar, you'll need a camera and a notebook.

PHYSICAL PREPARATION Start easy, start slow, and start walking around your neighborhood before you attempt a walk in the woods. Hiking can make muscles unaccustomed to exercise scream out in protest. Getting out of bed the day after a major hike can be a painful experience.

Don't overdo it when small children are along for the adventure. They will feel just as much accomplishment from a short walk in the woods as from a major hike. Stop often to talk and look around. After all, that's why you came. These are not overachiever events; they are family sharing times.

MENTAL PREPARATION Planning can be half the fun. Prepare family members by telling them several days ahead of the event where the family is going. Talk about it the day of the event and on the way.

Collecting waterfalls, pickle factories, bugs, and elephants without a jar is an opportunity to celebrate being together as a family. It is a chance to get to know better each other's strengths and weaknesses. It is a place to talk about and share meaningful life experiences.

What will your family collect?

8

A Fiddler on Your Roof

"Tradition! Tradition!" bellowed the actor who was playing the part of Tevya in the musical play *Fiddler on the Roof*. A fiddler follows him about as he sings. Then Tevya speaks the line upon which the entire play is based: "Without tradition our lives would be as—as shaky as a fiddler on a roof."

We had come to the ornate Fifth Avenue Theater to see the live presentation of *Fiddler on the Roof*. This was one of those special gifts to our children—gifts which didn't come wrapped in a box. We had spent too much and we were still too far back in the theater to see well, but we were enjoying ourselves anyway.

The play is about a Jewish family who lives in rural Russia. Tevya and Golda, his wife, have five daughters, three of whom are of marriageable age. During the play each one falls in love. The first chooses to marry a nice Jewish boy, a tailor. Her parents question her choice because he is so poor and because she made her choice without the aid of the village matchmaker, thus breaking with tradition. But her father sees his daughter's love for the tailor, and bends tradition a little to allow her to marry the man of her choice.

The second daughter falls in love with an itinerant teacher who also is Jewish; she, too, makes her own choice without the aid of the matchmaker. Once again, her parents reluctantly bend tradition.

The third falls in love with a young Russian soldier—a gentile. The girl's father is furious. "If I try to bend that far, I'll break!" he shouts. He disowns her because she has gone too far in violating her family's tradition.

In the last scene of the play, Tevya and his family flee their village as persecution of the Jewish people begins. In a last backward look over his shoulder, Tevya sees tradition, in the form of the fiddler, following just behind. Tevya beckons tradition to follow him to the new world.

Our family sat spellbound watching that play. Afterward the word *tradition* became—and still is to this day—a standard part of our family's vocabulary. Sometimes when the children asked Ed and I why we did things a certain way or made the decisions we did, we bellowed in our best baritone voices, "Tradition!"

Traditions Are Important

Traditions are an important part of family life. We can learn much from Tevya about when to bend tradition and when bending would destroy something valuable. Tradition builds strength into our families, a sense of the continuity of our family, and stability in a rapidly changing world.

Maybe the reason children and even adults like tradition so much is that it gives them something to anticipate. "Always" events, something we *always* do a certain time of year, or even "always" nights (I have a friend who *always* served spaghetti on Thursday nights) builds tradition into our families.

Children, particularly young ones, love repetition. They love to hear the same story over and over again. And they love events which they can look forward to year after year. In this chapter we will discuss celebrating everything, and in the next chapter we will talk about celebrating the big holidays— Christmas, Easter, and Thanksgiving.

This book is about passing your values on to your children through sharing experiences with them. One of the finest and most effective places to do this is through family events, both with the immediate and with extended family members.

We never have lived in the same area of the country as any members of our extended family until recently. Grandparents always have lived from a couple of hundred to more than a thousand miles away from us. Yet we believed that grandparents have something to contribute to their grandchildren's lives, particularly in the area of stability and traditions. So at least once a year, we packed the car, loaded kids, dogs, baby equipment, and whatever gear the current age of the children demanded, and drove across the country to spend time with their grandparents. We've driven without air conditioning across the Nevada desert. We've driven the same road when it was a sheet of ice for most of the trip. We did it because we felt it was important.

What a thrill it was for me to see Dad holding one of my little ones on his lap and to hear the child say, "Grandpa, tell us about the olden days."

"Yeah, tell us about when you built the giant slingshot," one of them almost always would say.

Grandpa would chuckle at the remembrance and then begin. Even though I had heard the story again and again as a child, I would find a chair, pull it up close, and listen to the story again.

When he finished the story, the kids would beg, "Tell us another story, Grandpa." And he would begin again.

Tradition—stories that are told over and over again, going again and again to Grandma and Grandpa's house, raiding the same cookie jar kept in the same place year after year, always having a special kind of birthday cake, building the value of family and tradition into your children, building self-esteem because the children themselves are the greatest value in your family. No one will treasure your children as much as the people in your family. Your children need to experience that sense of worth by spending time with family members.

Establishing Your Own Traditions

It is important to bring into your own family some of the traditions of each set of grandparents. Even though you will want to keep some of those old family traditions, it also is important to establish traditions that are just for your immediate family.

We've watched young couples try so hard to please their parents and extended families—by running here and there on holidays, birthdays, and anniversaries—that they never have taken the time to establish traditions just for their own children in their own home. At some point couples need to say, "No, Mom and Dad, we're not coming this year. We're going to have Christmas at home this time. It's time for us to establish our own traditions. We'll see you later on during the holidays." We've heard stories of their children's excitement from spending a special holiday at home with Mom and Dad.

As children grow older, it is important to modify or bend some of your traditions to fit the changing needs of your children and of the whole family. Flexibility is probably the most important characteristic in a parent. It is important to know when to let go of and when to keep a tradition. If your teenager has outgrown something you always have done, let it go, and don't make a federal case out of letting it go. Maybe it's time to stop giving him an Easter basket or insisting he spend every Sunday afternoon at Aunt Millie's just because you've always spent Sunday afternoons at Aunt Millie's.

I remember the year when I had been away on a long business trip until just two days before Thanksgiving. The thought of preparing a Thanksgiving dinner overwhelmed me, so we decided to go out for dinner. That's not very traditional in our family. But guess what? We all look back to that Thanksgiving as one of the best we ever had.

We chose a dining room high atop a hotel overlooking the city. The food was superb, and the variety endless. Everyone ate what he wanted. No one felt bad because someone was not eating Aunt Susie's sweet potato pie. And the real bonus was that there were no dishes to wash. We just sat and talked with each other. We enjoyed it so much that we have done it a couple of times since then. Who says Thanksgiving dinner has to be eaten at home with two dozen relatives?

Celebrating Everything

One way traditions can be built is by celebrating everything—and I mean everything. Celebrate with an elaborate party, or celebrate quietly, but celebrate life.

The following is a list of celebration ideas. But please don't stop here. Think of other days and ways you can celebrate life with your children. Make living at your house fun.

January

New Year's Day once was a time for holding open house and inviting friends to stop by, but those days probably are gone forever. For most families New Year's Day means football and football and football.

Even if viewing football was to be the order of the day, it always was more fun when we had family or friends to help us cheer. Even more fun was having someone who was cheering a rival team. Football on TV can be a shared experience if Dad or Mom, whichever is the fan, takes the time to explain to the kids what is happening and to instill his or her love of the game.

One of the things we tried to do on or around New Year's Day was to have a discussion that went something like this:

"What new thing did you learn or do in this last year?"

"I learned to ride a bike this year."

"I learned to sew."

"I learned to cross-country ski."

"I learned how to write a personality profile."

"Think now about some of the things we did together as a family that we never had done together. What were they?"

"Remember when we went out to the island where all those rabbits were running all over the place and there were holes everywhere?"

"Yeah. And remember we learned about the war that was started between the British and the Americans—over a pig?"

"Hey, remember how beautiful it was on the peninsula when we went to see all the wild rhododendrons? Man, they were all over the place."

"And remember how much fun we had riding our bikes through the woods and fields when we were camping at Fort Stevens Park?"

"You know what I remember about that? When we were reading together around the fire, the flying squirrels kept jumping back and forth through the trees."

And so we continued discussing the year's events, remembering the good times, evaluating what we had gained as a family, and sharing what had become important to us as a family.

The second question we asked was, "What would you like to learn to do in this new year?" This discussion became a time to set goals.

Martin Luther King Day: This new holiday is an important one. It is a time for discussing the contribution black Americans have made to our society. Because Martin Luther King, Jr., is a modern-day hero, it is possible to find a great deal of information about him. Television stations often replay footage of his life, his famous speeches, and his untimely death. You'll find many books about Dr. King in your local library.

Use this day to emphasize the value all people have in God's sight, regardless of their race or color. God loves all people and your kids need to know that.

Or use this day to play off Dr. King's "I Have a Dream" speech, and talk about your family's dreams and vision for the future.

Snow Day: Why not celebrate snow? Take time to play in the snow (if you live in an area where it snows). Plan a winter picnic of chili in an oversized thermos, sandwiches, hot chocolate, and cookies to wind up the meal. Find a sheltered place in the sunshine and enjoy being together as a family.

Play in the snow with the kids. Ride the sleds, even if your legs do hang out three feet behind. Build a snowman, even if he ends up lopsided and not much of an artistic achievement.

Some of our happiest memories are of times when my brothers' families joined us in Montana, and we spent the days trudging up hills, sometimes pulling a sled loaded with kids. Then everyone piled on the sled, flew down the hill, around the corner, across the bridge, and up the other side. Sometimes the sled spilled, and everyone laughed, dusted himself off, and climbed back on for the rest of the ride.

February

Groundhog Day: Research the legends associated with this day. Make sure your children understand that they are only legends and are just for fun. Before the day arrives, assign them the task of listening for interesting items about groundhogs from newspapers and television. They can share these. A prize could be given to the child who finds the most information about groundhogs or Groundhog Day.

Valentine's Day: I used to keep a set of Valentine cutouts—nice cardboard display items—from year to year and bring them out during Valentine's week. We'd attach them to the doors and windows around the house. On Valentine's Day we always had a special dinner. Each person gave the others a valentine, usually something they had made. Sometimes we had special heart-shaped cookies, a heart-shaped cake, or even a heart-shaped box of candy from the store.

One year we decided to find out the real meaning of Valentine's Day. So we read about St. Valentine. We learned that much of what we celebrate is myth, and that very little is known about Valentine himself. He was martyred on February 14, 270 A.D. The day has been celebrated since the seventh century, and because the day is around the same time birds begin mating, someone decided it would be a good day for young people to choose lovers. Thus the customs relating to hearts, cupids, and love were born.

Presidents' Day: This holiday affords your family a time for talking about the value of our governmental system. It can be a patriotic day of flag waving for your family. Sing patriotic songs. Read a story about George Washington or Abraham Lincoln. Cook a recipe from colonial or Civil War times.

Susan B. Anthony Day: Find out the contribution she made and share this information with the family. If possible have a Susan B. Anthony dollar to show the children.

March

Lion and Lamb Festival: Since March is supposed to either come in like a lion and leave like a lamb or vice versa, celebrate the event.

Discuss the ways in which Jesus Christ is like a lion or a lamb. Use a concordance to look up references. You might want to read a passage from *The Chronicles of Narnia* in which C. S. Lewis depicts Christ as the lion Aslan.

A great way to celebrate March is to purchase a new kite and go out together as a family to fly it. Real fun can be had with a two-handled model which can be made to dip and whirl. You can buy a kite for each person and hook them together in a chain. If you haven't visited a kite store for a while, you are in for a treat. Take the kids with you when you shop. You'll find beautiful kites of all shapes and sizes. A good one will last for years if properly cared for, so invest the money if you possibly can.

St. Patrick's Day: Every year a kind of madness settles in around the middle of March. The madness has a name—St. Patrick's Day. In our area the celebrating grows a little more lively every year, but you wouldn't want your family to participate in most of that celebrating.

You still can have fun together as a family. At our house, St. Patrick's Day called for a special meal celebration. We had corned beef and cabbage, something green to drink (usually lime drink), and something called Grasshopper Pie which is much better than it sounds.

The legends surrounding St. Patrick, for whom this day was named, are many. St. Patrick really did exist, and he really did live in Ireland although he was English. He was captured as a boy by the Irish. After six years he escaped. A series of miracles are said to have occurred when Patrick prayed. Eventually he returned to Ireland, where he was made a bishop.

First Day of Spring: If ever there was a day to celebrate, it is the coming of spring. Plant some flowers together; go for a walk; find a pond and see if there are any baby ducks or tadpoles yet; go to a park and run; play ball together; visit a farm and see the new lambs, colts, or calves.

A nearby research dairy allows visitors in its maternity barn. I still get a thrill when I see a newborn calf wobble its first few steps toward its mother. We always hoped we'd be there when a calf actually was being born. Once we arrived just minutes afterward, but we never were there at the actual moment of birth. Our kids had fun anyway. They liked to hang over the stall and let the calves suck on their fingers.

April

April Fools' Day: Who can start off April without at least one prank? Children love to celebrate this day. Help them think up fun, nondestructive pranks to pull on other family members. Let them dress up in polka dots and stripes—anything wild and crazy. Wear funny paper hats at dinner. Play silly, noisy games. Have fun!

Arbor Day: This is a day that almost goes unnoticed on our calendars. Traditionally, it has been set aside for the planting of trees. So in honor of the occasion, plant a tree. Your children may know more about this holiday than you do, as it is promoted through schools more than any other way. Find out if your kids have talked about it at school and let them teach you.

Time Change Day: This is the time change we all hate because we have to get up one hour earlier, and it usually happens on Sunday. Why not plan a special breakfast and serve it in an unusual spot in the house—like on Mom and Dad's bed, or before a roaring fire, or outside if you live in a warm area. Or perhaps you could take everyone out to breakfast before church.

May

May Day: This can be a delightful celebration, a time of giving. Our two children made little paper baskets with handles, filled them with garden flowers and maybe a cookie or a few candies, and then early in the morning hung them on the neighbors' doors. Then they rang the doorbell and ran.

Mother's Day: This is one of the big holidays of the year. Let the children decide what they will do to honor their mother. Dad needs to help make their wishes come true. If they are too young to be aware of the specialness of this day, he also needs to talk with them about Mother's Day and help the children find a way to show how much they value their mother.

This must be a tough holiday for single moms. Let the children surprise you, even though you may be aware of what they are planning, and even if their plans may result in a messy house—something that you don't need in your busy schedule. You even may have to clean up after them. Be truly grateful for their clumsy efforts. As time goes on, they will treasure you more, and they will begin to realize what you have given of yourself to make their lives good. In time they will find a better way to reward you.

Single fathers need to encourage their children to honor their mother.

Memorial Day is a day for remembering. The Apostle Paul encouraged Timothy to remember what he had been taught as a youth. Memorial Day can be a time for remembering those who've lived before us. This is a good day to look at old photos and learn more about your family's history. It also is a good time for taking children to visit graves of loved ones and talking about those who've gone to heaven ahead of us.

Many towns have Memorial Day parades with a lot of military activity. Explain what this is all about to your children. Go on a picnic. Spend this day together getting to know one another better so that you are building your own memories.

June

Flag Day: I don't know why I never bought a flag for our family to fly on special holidays. It is a fun thing to do and a reminder about this special day. This is a day set aside to commemorate the June 14, 1777, adoption by the Continental Congress of a resolution to make the stars and stripes the official flag of the United States.

Buy a flag, recite the pledge of allegiance together, and sing "The National Anthem." Talk about why we stand at attention when this song is played. Once again, your school-aged children probably will know more about this holiday than you do. Learn from them.

Father's Day: This is Dad's special day, and now it is Mom's privilege to lead her children in honoring their father. Plan a special meal of his favorite foods, serve him breakfast in bed, or take him out to eat. Learn a poem or a Scripture verse about fathers and recite that to him as a gift. One time Mark learned to recite all the books of the New Testament in order as a surprise gift for his dad. Dad was very pleased, and Mark kept the knowledge.

In a home headed by a single mother, children should be encouraged to spend the day with their father, if that is appropriate. Single moms need to be supportive of the children's father. Nothing good will come from instilling bitterness in the children's hearts toward their father no matter what has happened in the past.

Have a devotional time and talk about the fatherhood of God. Help your children see God as a tender papa who loves them and expects obedience from them. Teach your children to respect both their earthly father and their Heavenly Father.

First Day of Summer: Celebrate the longest day of the year. Go on a picnic, even an impromptu picnic if it is a weekday. Just pick up dinner and take it to a park. Picnics do not have to consist of traditional picnic food. It is possible to make a picnic from your regular dinner or you can stop at a fast-food place to eat. We used to do that a lot, and after a few minutes outdoors, frayed nerves disappeared and cranky kids began to have fun playing with each other.

Why not let the kids stay up until sunset regardless of how late it is?

July

Independence Day: The only holiday in July is Independence Day. If you bought a flag for Flag Day, fly it again. If you allow your children to have their own fireworks, then help them purchase them and supervise their use. Watch the neighbors' fireworks, or go to the city's fireworks display.

Talk about what it means to be a free people, and give thanks to God that we are free. Discuss the cost of our freedom and how we can maintain it by being good citizens.

Spend the day with family and friends. Use the time to draw closer together as a family.

August

Friendship Day: August is the only month without a traditional holiday, so someone invented Friendship Day. If you never have celebrated this day, then here's your chance. Think of something to do to encourage friendship—having a block party in your neighborhood, sending homemade cards to friends, or letting the children invite a special friend to spend the day or night. Talk together about the value of a good friend.

September

Labor Day is the last holiday of the summer. It is the last chance for your family to do something together before the new school year begins. Why not do something special, such as a short trip, a picnic, a bike ride, or something you have been wanting to do for a long time.

This would be an excellent time to discuss the upcoming school year. You could talk together about your expectations of grades to be earned. You could pray together about the new teachers. You could discuss any fears kids might be having about the new school year. You even might suggest some events or awards for excellent grades, or just something for them to anticipate as they are working at school.

Grandparents' Day: This is another fairly new holiday, and a worthwhile one. Help your children think of ways to honor their grandparents. They could call their grandparents and express their love. Or perhaps they could make or buy a special card. A handmade thank-you book, flowers, or a time of special prayer for their grandparents would be special gifts.

Beginning of Fall: Celebrate fall with a leaf-raking-and-burning party, if it is allowed in your area. Go for a walk and kick the leaves. Gather colored leaves, and award a prize to the person finding the most beautiful leaf. Pick apples and let the kids help you make an apple pie. Sit on a hillside and listen to the quiet of an autumn day. Watch for flights of geese and other birds headed south for the winter.

October

Columbus Day: Read together about Columbus. Trace his route on a world map or globe. Discuss what it would be like to venture to a place where no one ever has been. Compare his journey to that of the first astronauts to the moon. Read in the Bible about Abraham starting off for a country where he had never been. Lead children in talking about trust in God.

Because Columbus was Italian, serve an Italian dinner. Use world maps as place mats, and a toy boat for a centerpiece.

United Nations Day: Serve an international dinner—first course from one country, main course from another, and so on. Decorate your table with flags from many nations.

Explain how the United Nations was born. Talk about the Scripture verse displayed in the lobby of the United Nations: ". . . they shall beat their swords into plowshares, and their spears into pruning hooks; nation shall not lift up sword against nation, neither shall they learn war any more" (Isaiah 2:4 RSV).

Time Change: Because everyone can sleep an hour later on Sunday morning, let them stay up an hour longer on Saturday night, and do something together in that extra hour. Read a story, have a pillow fight, go out for hot chocolate, or make popcorn. Talk about time as God's gift to us, and how we need to make the best use of our time. (That includes taking time for fun with our kids.)

Halloween: When our children were little not much thought was given to the occult aspect of Halloween. It was simply a fun night for the kids to dress up in costumes and go to the neighbors' houses. But today parents need to give serious thought to this holiday. With so much occult activity and satanic worship in our country and others, we need to be very careful not to open the door to any of this.

And yet the neighbors' kids are celebrating and yours will feel badly if they can't. Substitute and do it with so much style that your kids never will notice they are not celebrating like everyone else. A hobo party is fun. Everyone dresses like a hobo. Serve stew in a tin can. Give a prize for the best hobo costume. Have an All Saints party where children dress up like a Bible character. Have a harvest festival and visit a pumpkin farm. Eat pumpkin ice cream afterward. Take your kids to the store the day after Halloween and let them buy a generous supply of candy, which now is being sold at a discounted price.

November

Election Day: Have a red, white, and blue theme at the dinner table. Talk about the responsibility of American citizens to vote. Talk about the relationship between being a good citizen and a good Christian.

Veterans Day: Fly your American flag again today. Talk about the purpose of this day. Research some great American heroes, and talk about what they did for this country. Discuss people in your family who are veterans. Or better still, if possible, invite those people to come and share their experiences with your children.

Thanksgiving: We'll talk about this in the next chapter.

December

Bill of Rights Day: Did you know that such a day exists? The Bill of Rights of the American Constitution is probably the most important document of its kind ever formulated. If your children are old enough, read the Bill of Rights and tell them why each point is important. Give them the Christian perspective on each point.

Winter: Have a winter festival. Let your children cut paper snowflakes from tissue paper and post them all over your windows. Let them buy a new winter hat or mittens. Make popcorn balls to look like snowballs, or pop some corn and string it in preparation for Christmas. Talk about this being the shortest day of the year. Explain how short the days are in places like Alaska and Lapland which are nearer the Arctic Circle. Get out a seed catalog and discuss what you will plant when it is spring.

Christmas: We'll talk about this in the next chapter.

That takes us through the year with dozens of ideas for celebrating everything on the calendar. There are still more occasions to celebrate as well.

Birthdays: One family has a banner for each person in the family and flies it outside on birthdays and other days that are special to that person.

   First day of school
   Last day of school
   Anniversaries—parents, grandparents
   Graduation—fly the banner of the one graduating
   Special awards won by family members
   Favorite team wins
   When you make a special purchase—such as a new car
   First snowfall
   Leaving home—don't forget the banner
   Coming home again—yellow ribbon or a banner

Life is so short, and the time we have with our children is even shorter. Why shouldn't it be fun to be together? Why shouldn't we celebrate everything? In doing so, we may find we are celebrating life itself.

9

Family Seasoning

I watched as Wendy searched under the tree for the special gift she had made her daddy. At last she found it. Crossing the floor, she handed it to him and with eyes shining said, "Merry Christmas, Daddy. I made this for you." She stood on tiptoe and kissed him, and then stood back to watch him open the gift.

Then it was Mark's turn to present a gift. He carried it to Wendy and said, "This is for you, from me." She thanked him, hugged him (he backed away a little at that), and began opening the gift while he stood watching with his hands in his pockets. She "oohed" and "aahed" and said the appropriate things.

Throughout the evening, each of us found the special gifts we had chosen for each other and presented them one by one. It took a long time, but as the evening wore on the children were more eager to give what they had purchased for the others than they were to receive their own presents.

We never did allow them to rip and tear into all of the gifts under the tree all at once. Sometimes we even stopped opening gifts for a while and had a late supper. Even when the extended family was able to spend Christmas together, we never did have a free-for-all with the gifts. It was a tradition passed down from my childhood and handed to our children.

Giving Gifts

Learning to give is an important value. Even when children are very young they can begin to learn how to give. Christmas is an excellent time to teach them.

We taught them through a family outing evening in which we took the children Christmas shopping, usually in a large department store. Ed took one of the children, and I took the other, and then halfway through the evening we switched kids and finished the shopping. They really looked forward to this evening.

My friend Carol tells a delightful story about a similar shopping excursion. Her husband was shopping with one of their children when he realized that the little girl he was holding by the hand had grown very quiet. Nothing was said, but somehow he understood what she was thinking. Quietly he reached into his back pocket, took a five-dollar bill from his wallet, and pressed it into her hand without a word. Soon a happy little girl was purchasing a very special gift.

Christmas is a special time for all of us, but especially for children. It is a time for learning about the depth of God's love for His creation in that He gave us the best that heaven had to offer, His Son, Jesus.

The Problem of Santa

The problem of what Christians tell their kids about Santa doesn't really need to be much of a problem at all. Kids believe what they want to believe, at least for a time.

When one of our kids wanted to know where puppies came from, I explained as simply and carefully as I could. Whereupon the child responded, "Huh uh!" No way would that child believe the truth. It was just too unbelievable for the young mind.

The same thing happened when the kids asked me if Santa Claus existed. As sensitively as possible, I explained that many people do believe in Santa; I didn't want them to rush out and offend half the parents in the neighborhood by telling their children there is no Santa. I explained to them that in our family he isn't the important part about Christmas. Jesus is. "But, Mom, is there really a Santa Claus?" they persisted.

"Well, no, there probably isn't."

At that I received the same reply, "Huh uh. I think there is."

I didn't argue the point. I just dropped it.

In all of our family's Christmas celebrations the emphasis was upon the birth of Jesus. Over and over we sought ways to make Christ the focus of our celebration.

One of the things that helps to diffuse the Santa Claus issue is to find the origin of the legend of Santa. A little digging at the library will unearth some interesting information. But to save you some time, let me share what I learned from my research.

St. Nicholas was bishop of the church of Myra. He was born about 280 A.D. in Patara. Both cities were located in present-day Turkey.

Nicholas was like any other boy of his time except that his parents were wealthy, and he inherited this wealth when they died. It has become difficult to distinguish between fact and legend regarding Nicholas. But the legends tell us that the young Nicholas was very generous toward children, young maidens in distress, and sailors.

A story which appears repeatedly is that Nicholas gave part of his wealth as dowries for three girls whose father was unable to provide them himself. Nicholas gave the money to the girls by throwing a bag of gold through their window and making a quick escape. When he left money for the first two daughters he slipped away successfully, and no one knew who had provided the dowries. But when he tried it a third time he was caught, and everyone knew that he was the giver of the gifts.

Often three gold balls are included in pictures depicting St. Nicholas. These are symbolic of the three golden gifts for the three dowries.

His history also is filled with stories of how he rescued sailors from untimely deaths at sea. He became the patron saint of sailors. His acts of generosity and the stories of miracles he performed were carried from port to port by the sailors. After a time people began to give gifts secretly to others, saying they came from St. Nicholas.

Later children began to leave their shoes filled with hay and carrots outside the door for St. Nicholas's horse, North Star. At last St. Nicholas's birthday, December 6, became the feast day that still is celebrated in Europe. It is on this day that European children receive their Christmas presents.

From central Europe the legend was carried to Scandinavian countries. The Lapps added the story of Nicholas coming on a reindeer or in a sleigh pulled by reindeer.

The legend of St. Nicholas came with the Dutch to New Amsterdam in New York State. They called him Sinter Klaus. But it was not until much later in the early nineteenth century that Santa Claus came into being when Clement Moore penned his famous poem *The Night Before Christmas*. The poem's illustrator faithfully followed the descriptions of St. Nicholas as narrated by Moore.

Everywhere American soldiers went they carried the legend of Santa Claus with them. Santa Claus came to the battlefields of the Pacific and Korea in a bright red suit trimmed with white fur.

Today children all over the world eagerly await the coming of Santa Claus.

Here are some discussion questions you might ask after telling your children this story:

1. What do you think the original St. Nicholas might think if he could see what people believe about him now?
2. Do you think he would be surprised?
3. Do you think he might be sad?
4. St. Nicholas was a good, kind bishop who cared about people. Has any of that attitude survived in our Christmas celebrations today?
5. If you could talk to Nicholas, what would you want to ask him?

Help your children to see that legends grow up around well-known people and that because Nicholas lived so long ago, there are many, many legends surrounding him. Help them to appreciate who he really was—a kind and loving man who reached out to the needy. Help them see that Nicholas had the love of Christ in his heart.

Emphasize Jesus, give your children information about the real person the mythical Santa is based on, and ignore the modern version of Santa. Your kids will figure it out when they are ready.

Emphasizing Jesus

There are dozens of ways to emphasize Jesus in Christmas celebrations. One way is to have a birthday party for Jesus. Even the smallest toddlers can relate to a birthday party. It was always a fun thing to do at our house.

We decorated a cake together, put birthday candles on it, and then on Christmas day sang happy birthday to Jesus, blew out the candles, and ate the cake. I don't remember ever being asked how Jesus was going to get His piece of cake.

Advent

Another meaningful observance is Advent, which begins the Sunday after Thanksgiving. At the public library you'll find many ideas and ways of celebrating this holiday. For several years we celebrated Advent, and the children enjoyed it very much. Let me tell you how we did it.

To celebrate this holiday you'll need an Advent wreath with five candles. You can purchase them at church supply stores, or you can construct your own by inserting candles into a Styrofoam circle which has been covered with sprigs of evergreen or holly.

If you construct your own advent wreath, make it a family holiday project. Send everyone out to search for greens or let them help purchase them from a store. There are many opinions about the proper color of the Advent candles. Some use four red ones around the outside and a white one in the middle. Others use pink candles around the outside and a purple one in the middle. But the color really doesn't matter.

In the Advent service we used, the first candle represented the prophets who foretold Christ's birth; the second represented Mary, the mother of Christ; the third represented Joseph; the fourth, the shepherds; and the one in the middle, of course, represented Christ.

Because we have four people in our family, each of us had a turn to light a candle. In larger families, the oldest child can light the first candle, and the youngest the last. Or children can take turns during the weeks of Advent. On Christmas Day we all lit the Christ candle with our four burning candles.

Here is an outline for a short celebration to accompany the lighting of each candle.

First Week: Prophecy Candle

It is important that your children know Christ's birth was prophesied long before He came. He did not just suddenly show up on the scene to live thirty-three years and then disappear. His coming was planned by God from the beginning of all things. Here is a partial list of Scriptures which prophesied His coming:

> Genesis 3:15
> Isaiah 7:14
> Isaiah 9:1, 2, 6, 7
> Isaiah 52:13—53:12
> Malachi 3:1

Read several of these Scriptures together, and talk about what you have read. Then one person should light the first candle. Sing a Christmas carol or two. Then blow out the candle and leave the wreath where the whole family can see it.

Second Week: Mary Candle

The second candle is for Mary, the mother of Jesus. Read together the story of Gabriel's announcement to her in Luke 1:26–38. Help your children to understand that Mary was being given the highest honor any woman ever could have—to become the mother of the Saviour of the world.

Light the prophecy candle again, and have a second family member light the candle for Mary. Then sing appropriate Christmas carols.

This would be a great story for the family to dramatize. Put on bathrobes and towels for turbans. Let one person be the angel who announced the good news to Mary.

Talk about what happened to Mary. Why did the angel tell her not to be afraid? How do family members think Mary felt? Why was Mary so willing to become the mother of Jesus? If your children are old enough, talk about the stigma attached to this event. Explain that Mary, although engaged, was not yet married. Explain what that would mean in her culture. Pray together and thank God for sending Jesus.

Third Week: Joseph Candle

The third candle represents Joseph. Read Matthew 1:18–25 in which Joseph is told about Christ's birth.

Have family members relight the first two candles, and then have a third family member light the Joseph candle. Sing appropriate carols. Once again, family members could act out the story.

Discuss how Joseph must have felt when he saw the angel. Be sure your children understand that Joseph was the earthly father of Jesus, that God entrusted Mary and Jesus into his hands, but that God was the Heavenly Father of Jesus. You will have to tailor this discussion according to the ages of your children.

Fourth Week: Shepherds Candle

Read Luke 2:8–20, the story of the angel's pronouncement to the shepherds in the fields.

Relight all the candles. (You may have to replace some of them by now.) Sing appropriate Christmas carols. .

Talk together about why the shepherds were in the fields. Emphasize that they were the first to greet the new baby lying in a manger. Discuss their humble attitude, our attitude toward Jesus, and the importance of adoring Jesus Christ.

Spend time together praying. Encourage the children to make statements of adoration to Christ.

Christmas Day

Read the passage about the birth of Christ in Luke 2:1–7.

Relight all four candles and then lift them from their places. Together as a family, light the center candle, which represents Christ. Reinsert the other candles in their places. Sing Christmas carols together and rejoice that Christ is born.

Pray together and give thanks for God's great gift, Jesus Christ. Let the candles burn throughout dinner if you are doing your Advent celebration along with a meal. If not, put the wreath in a safe place and let the candles burn for a time.

Other Advent Ideas

Some families celebrate Advent with a Bible-reading program similar to the one listed above, but instead of using candles they use a nativity scene.

The first week the empty manger is placed in a prominent position—low enough so the littlest ones can see it. The idea is to move the figures toward the manger scene a little each week. The first week (prophecy) use no figures because prophecy is foretelling something no one has seen yet. Read the same Scriptures and talk about prophecy in general. Talk about the people who waited and waited for the Messiah.

The second week place Mary somewhere in the room, but not at the manger. Place an angel nearby when you read the story of the announcement. Use the same carols and readings.

The third week place Joseph near Mary, and the angel figure nearby. Read the Scriptures relating to Joseph and the angel's announcement to him. Sing the appropriate carols and pray together.

The fourth week you will need to deviate from the Advent-candle plan. Read and talk about Joseph and Mary's journey to Bethlehem. Let the children move the figures closer and closer to the manger throughout the devotional time. Then finally place them in the manger.

On Christmas Day let the children place the Christ Child in the manger. Read the appropriate Scriptures and sing carols. Then place the shepherds somewhere in the room and bring the angel figures to make their announcement. After this bring the shepherds into the scene as well. If you have time, read the Scriptures given above.

Reserve the wise men for Epiphany, which is described next.

Epiphany

Epiphany, celebrated January 6, is the traditional holiday which celebrates the revealing of Christ to the gentiles, represented by the wise men from the east. In some countries this is the day for giving gifts. In many places it is considered the conclusion of the Christmas season.

Our family celebrated Epiphany a few times by leaving our Christmas tree up until this day. In the evening we gathered together and read all the Christmas cards we had received during the holidays. Sometimes we had been too busy to read them carefully. Now we took the time. We also chose the cards we considered the prettiest, the funniest, the most meaningful, and so on.

We usually played our favorite Christmas records once again before putting them away for the year. And we ate the Christmas goodies during the evening.

It is a lovely way to conclude the Christmas season. The next morning I took down the tree and packed everything related to Christmas.

If you used nativity figures to celebrate Advent, read the Scriptures relating to the wise men. As you read, move the figures closer and closer to the nativity scene. You will have to explain to the children that the wise men probably did not come to Bethlehem until as much as two years after Christ was born. And as far as singing, what else could you sing but "We Three Kings of Orient Are."

Slowing Down

Is there a man, woman, boy, or girl alive who does not love Christmas? And yet Christmas can be a time of extreme stress if parents do not slow down and enjoy their children and their homes during this season. Do everything you can to keep a calm atmosphere that honors Christ throughout the holidays.

We talked in the previous chapter about the importance of establishing your own traditions in your own home. This is vitally important at Christmas. Take time to be in your own home at Christmas, and to share your values about God's gift to the world in the person of his Son, Jesus.

A fun thing we did as the children were growing up was to buy them each a special Christmas ornament each year. Year by year it was so much fun to see the kids' collection of ornaments grow, and to think back to the year each ornament represented. If you do this, when the child is grown and leaves home, the ornament collection goes with him as a start for a new home and a new set of traditions.

This year, for the first time, one set of ornaments is gone

from our tree. They will hang on Wendy's Christmas tree in Belgium. I wonder where they will hang in the future.

One family shared their delightful way to celebrate Christmas Eve. Because they are far from family and friends and they want to avoid being lonely, they take their children to a Chinese restaurant on Christmas Eve. They also take along the small gifts that have come from aunts, uncles, cousins, and grandparents. The children, now teenagers, open these gifts at the restaurant.

After the meal the family boards a ferry and rides across Puget Sound to see the city all aglitter with Christmas lights. They go home very late and then on Christmas morning they celebrate their own family's gift giving.

Easter

Perhaps the most important holiday of the year for a Christian family is Easter. Without the resurrection we have no hope and no future. But because He lives, we can face the future. In a war-infested, poverty-ridden, disease-suffering world, our children need hope.

Easter can be a shared experience through which we emphasize again and again the importance of our relationship with God. We value Jesus Christ. We value the cross and the finished work of Calvary. We need to pass those values on to our children.

Sometime during the holiday, sit down together and read the Easter story. If the children are able to read, let them participate. If they are unable to read, choose a Bible storybook that is simple enough for them to understand. As you share this reading time together, remember that the story you are reading is the most important one in the Bible—the most important one in all of history. Take time for it.

Easter Bunnies

What we tell our children about Santa Claus probably lays the groundwork for what we tell them about the Easter Bunny. If we value the Jesus Christ of Christmas, we probably will value the Jesus Christ of Easter. He is the important factor in the Easter celebration. He is the focal point.

The difference between the Easter Bunny and Santa Claus is that Santa Claus is based on a religious historical figure. The Easter Bunny has no such basis. It is hard to find any significant spiritual meaning in this symbol for Easter.

Once again, the best thing to do is to focus on Jesus and ignore the other symbols of Easter. It is good to talk about new life as evidenced by chicks and ducklings. It is all right to purchase new clothes for Easter as a symbol of newness, if it is not overdone. After all, Jesus came and died to bring us new life.

Lenten Observances

The Lenten period can be a special time for our families. It can be a time for giving up something so that someone else can be blessed. Many people sacrifice something for the good of others. Why not discuss with your children what sacrificial gift they might like to make to bless others? Perhaps your family can choose to help one of the many programs which feed the hungry.

Let your children decide what they will give up as a sacrifice. They may decide to give up ice cream, and give the money to the needy. It could be their allowances or part of their allowances. Perhaps they will choose to work to contribute to the sacrificial offering. Decide together as a family and then work to help, support, and remind each other of what you are trying to do.

Traditions of Easter

Coloring Eggs: An Easter highlight for our family was coloring eggs. Here creativity reigned as king. We always did it together as a family project.

On Easter afternoon, after church and dinner, Ed and I played in the yard with the kids and hid the eggs everywhere. We had a shaggy gray poodle that often gave away the hiding places. The children never tired of having us hide the eggs or of hiding them themselves. It was a fun time of shared experience for our family. We weren't trying to communicate any heavy messages. We were just playing with our kids.

Easter Baskets: We always fixed Easter baskets for the kids.

After they went to bed on the evening before Easter, I filled and decorated Easter baskets. There were no shared experiences here until the next day when we helped them eat the contents of their baskets.

New Clothes: New Easter clothes are traditional for some people. I think it is emphasized far too much. Many, many people cannot buy new clothes. It is far better to have an attitude which says each time we go to church, "Today we are going to God's house and His house is one of the most important places we go. So let's try to look as neat and clean as possible." The important thing isn't our clothes, but an attitude of the heart which says, "I want to be at my best for God and His house."

We always tried to make going to church something special every week. We helped the children dress to look the best they could. But when they became teens they often wore to church what I considered play clothes. We had learned not to get too excited about unimportant matters. It really doesn't matter how long or short a kid's hair is. It really doesn't matter what he chooses to wear to church. What's important is that *he is in church.* And it may not be important to you, but looking like everyone else his age is *very* important to him.

Going to church on Easter: Church should be a regular part of your life-style, and Easter should be no different. It is merely the emphasis of the day—a celebration of resurrection—that is different.

Easter Lilies: In our church, families buy Easter lilies in memory of loved ones. The flowers remain in the church through the Easter celebration and then are taken home. Perhaps you could make it a family project to buy an Easter lily in memory of someone you love for your church.

Thanksgiving Day

A little more than 300 years ago our forefathers stood on the shores of a new land and gave thanks to God for keeping them through the previous year.

Consider all that has happened in those 300 years. Today our land is teeming with people, industry, health facilities, automobiles, homes, and thousands of wonderful things. We have much for which to thank God. We should value God's good gifts to us in America, and we should teach our children to value them as well. Thanksgiving is a time to do that.

Review the story of the Pilgrims by getting a storybook from the library. Or perhaps your children will be able to tell you much about the holiday because they have studied it in school. Let them share with you.

A delightful film now available in video is *An American Tail* which tells the story of a Russian mouse family which immigrates to America. At one point all the mice are pouring onto Ellis Island. In the background plays a song composed of the words engraved on the Statue of Liberty:

Give me your tired, your poor,
Your huddled masses yearning to breathe free,
The wretched refuse of your teeming shore,
Send these, the homeless, tempest-tost to me,
I lift my lamp beside the golden door!
                                          EMMA LAZARUS

Although it is a fantasy story and is not about people, help your children understand what it was like for people to come to this country from poverty, oppression, and fear, and help them give thanks.

Viewing this video together, and then talking about what it means to live in America and how hard some people have had to work to get here, will give you a chance to share your values about life in this country.

Many churches and civic organizations have programs not only for contributing to needy families, but also for cooking dinner for these people. What a learning experience it would be for your children if they could stand beside you while you work at a shelter, helping feed the hungry. They will know instantly that you value people and because you do, you are giving back some of your life and time to those who are less fortunate.

Thanksgiving should be a time for sharing. Look around your community to find lonely people—singles with or without children—and invite them in to share the day. Every person who sits at your table brings a new insight about life.

If you are single, consider inviting other singles, or you even could invite a married couple to join you for dinner.

Attend a traditional family gathering, or as we said in an earlier chapter, maybe you want to forego the traditional feast and go out to dinner.

Giving Thanks

Whatever you do, make giving thanks a part of your celebration. If your church has a Thanksgiving Day service, take the kids and attend it. Talk afterward about how to give thanks to God. Pray together and, by your example, teach your children to pray prayers of thanksgiving to God.

The well-seasoned family is a joyful, happy family celebrating the important holidays in a way that pleases God because it puts the emphasis where it belongs—on Him.

10

A Night on the Town

"This is a model of the funeral barge of King Tut," Mark told someone standing nearby. "And this is a game board he used."

The man he was talking to stood back and looked at this nine-year-old boy who knew so much about Tutankhamen, the boy king of Egypt.

Several months earlier we had heard that the King Tut exhibit was coming to Seattle, and had ordered tickets at that time. There was a lot of excitement about this exhibit coming to town and a lot of information was available—TV specials, books, and pamphlets.

Because both Ed and I are interested in history, and the history of Egypt is so closely tied to our biblical roots, we decided to learn all we could about King Tut and Egypt, and to involve the children in our learning process.

By the time the exhibit arrived in town, they were well versed in Eygptian history in general and King Tut in particular. We stood in line for a long, long time; finally our group was let in to see the opulent treasure of a fabulously wealthy king who died when he was only seventeen years old.

That cultural event stands out as a highlight in the children's lives. But we shared dozens of other fun cultural experiences. Some of them I have already mentioned—seeing Dickens's *A Christmas Carol*, *The Nutcracker Ballet*, and the Shakespearean Festival.

Some cultural events are expensive. But if you look at them as an investment—an investment you cannot lose—then the price tag doesn't seem quite so high. It is a matter of priorities.

Better to have one really spectacular event in the children's growing-up years than dozens of trips to McDonald's.

Susan is a single parent whose job often takes her away from home. She decided that about every ten weeks she and her two daughters would do something really spectacular. Her first spectacular activity was to rent a limousine for a day. The limo picked them up and took them to brunch at a wonderful restaurant right on the water with a view of the city. After brunch they went to a professional football game, but because they arrived too early for the game, the driver took them on a tour of the city, stopping anywhere they wished to take pictures. Then they went to the stadium and watched the game. It helped so much that their favorite team won. After the game the driver took them home.

I asked Susan why she chose this very creative idea. She said that because her work takes her away so much, she wanted this special time with her girls. She used honorarium funds from her speaking engagements to pay for this event. Her children are precious to her and are more important than the work which takes her away so often. By sharing the proceeds from her trips with them, she is, in essence, letting them share in her work. These girls know they are highly valued by their mother.

In some families the children work to contribute money toward a special event. Those children probably appreciate the event even more than children who merely are handed a ticket.

Decide Which Cultural Events Are Important to You

Before you can pass on your value of a cultural event, you have to decide what you value and why. In some families children grow up without ever going to see even one art show or traveling exhibit because it is not something their parents value. That's all right. Each family has a different value system. Different is not wrong; it's just different. Many families value sporting events above cultural events. That's all right too. But being exposed to cultural events stretches our children and gives them a broader view of the world. It is something worth considering when deciding how your family's limited entertainment budget will be spent.

You must determine when your children are mature enough to attend cultural events. If you wait until they are teens to introduce them to ballet, opera, and plays, they probably won't be interested. But at the same time, it can be miserable trying to take a two-year-old toddler to an art museum.

Any metropolitan area offers more cultural events than you possibly can find time to attend. But if you do not live in a metropolitan area, you can still be exposed to some cultural events.

I grew up in a very small town in Montana where the only cultural center, if you could call it that, was the local theater. But just thirty-five miles away in Butte there were often programs featuring truly famous people. My parents did not have a season ticket to these events, but I did manage to attend some of them. I remember hearing Yehudi Menuhin play the violin. Afterward my violin teacher took me backstage to meet him. I've never forgotten the thrill of that moment.

I also had the privilege of taking piano lessons from a Latvian refugee who lived in our town. She had been a concert pianist in Europe and was a superb musician.

Whenever our school music department showed films of operas and ballet, I sat entranced. I often listened to the Metropolitan Opera on radio on Saturdays while helping with housework. I may have been an unusual young person to have so much interest in these things, but that is not the point I am trying to make. The point is that even though I lived in a town of 4500 people high in the mountains of Montana, and even though it was thirty-five miles to the nearest town which also had little to offer culturally, it was possible to learn about these things simply by taking advantage of what *was* available.

Look around you if you are isolated in some small town and see what is available. Often the cultural events in rural America are centered around the ethnic group which established the town. Some wonderful traditions are handed down from generation to generation. Find out about them and begin to learn from your neighbors.

With the advent of video, it is possible to bring into our homes some of the best cultural events in the world. It is simply a matter of choosing to see those kinds of videos rather than a steady diet of Walt Disney movies.

Some Cultural Events to Consider

BALLET　Some people consider ballet a feminine interest. It is a beautiful art form often performed in soft, exquisite, flowing costumes. But it is more than that. It is also athletic ability at its finest. Dancers must be conditioned to a level of Olympic readiness. The leaps, lifts, spins, and stretches of the dance are truly athletic achievements.

One day I passed by a TV set and noticed that a male ballet dancer was performing on the screen. I had no idea who it was, but I was galvanized by the power and strength of this performer. I stopped to watch. Soon I realized that no one could leap that high—except Mikhail Baryshnikov. Baryshnikov is a powerful athlete who combines his athletic prowess with the ability to relate a story through the movement of dance and facial expressions.

Several ballets are classics, and since you probably will not be going on a regular basis, why not choose those? I already have mentioned *The Nutcracker Ballet*. The other great classic, of course, is *Swan Lake*. It will help your children understand what is happening if they know the plot of the story. Do a little research ahead of time, and explain to them what is happening.

OPERA　Opera is another great art form that is not understood by many people because few ever take the time to find out about it. Opera, as you probably know, is a dramatic play which is sung rather than spoken.

Because so many operas are performed in languages other than English, it becomes impossible to understand for those who speak only English. If you want to see an opera in a language other than English, you will have to do some studying about the opera ahead of time. Whether it's in English or not, it still is a good idea to learn the opera's plot.

The only opera we ever took our almost-grown kids to was *The Marriage of Figaro* by Mozart. We all enjoyed it greatly. It was about the time *Amadeus*, the movie about Mozart's life, was released. By putting the two events together, the children gained a rich sense of the genius of Mozart.

A while ago Wendy and I had the wonderful privilege of going backstage at the Seattle Opera on dress rehearsal night and helping the singers with their costumes and makeup for the opera *Rigoletto*. It was great fun to help lace the ladies into heavily brocaded velvet gowns and to watch how nervous they were about their performance.

PLAYS I've already mentioned some of the plays we took our children to see—Shakespearean theater, *A Christmas Carol*, and *Fiddler on the Roof*. I wish we could have gone to more, but we, too, worked with a limited budget.

There were other less expensive events that we discovered. Several times we went to an inexpensive children's theater and watched with amazement the very creative portrayal of some well-known children's stories.

Many times when we were traveling we discovered theater in the park. Fort Worth, Texas, has a fine Shakespearean theater in a park every week throughout the summer and it's free. Just get there early to find a good place to sit on the grass.

Once in Montana, in a town even smaller than my hometown, we encountered theater produced by university students in the local park. We saw *Cyrano de Bergerac*. The creative set changes in that production were worth staying to see. Never mind the mosquitoes which were trying to drain us dry, never mind the coolness of the mountain air. We were lost in the story of Cyrano de Bergerac.

A word of warning. Be very careful about live theater. Know what you will be seeing and try to find out how it will be interpreted. We had seen quite a bit of Shakespeare before we went to an outdoor presentation in our city. The way in which the actors were portraying this particular play—a comedy— was so lewd that we decided this was not for us, and we left.

In our city there is also a fine Christian drama group which we have seen perform a number of times. It was they who introduced our family to C. S. Lewis's *The Lion, the Witch and the Wardrobe*. It was done without costumes or sets as pantomime.

You also may find reader's theater in your area. This is theater in which actors sitting on stools read the play with such expression and style that you may be convinced you are seeing the action. It teaches what can be done with the voice alone, and encourages your young people to learn to speak well with expression.

SYMPHONY Many Christian parents are concerned when their children become avid rock music fans. As we all know, rock music often portrays many values that are not espoused by Christian families—drug use, occultish practices, sexual insinuation, and more.

Rock music is here to stay. There's not much we can do to insulate our young people from it. The best thing we can do is give them something inside that will keep them from caving in to the pressure to conform, which is pushing on them from the outside. If what's inside is as strong as what's outside, they will not give in to pressure.

We need to introduce a love of good music to our children. When our children were infants and I put them down for naps, I often turned on a classical music radio station to cover neighborhood noises. In one home where we lived, the young people next door practiced for their rock band in their garage. We needed something to cover up the loud drumming at nap time.

We also encouraged our children to take music lessons for several reasons. One reason was the discipline a young person must develop to learn to play an instrument. It's every day, every day, every day—practice, practice, practice. Another reason is the personal achievement a young person feels when he finally accomplishes being able to play. One more reason is that in the process, the young person is exposed to a wide variety of excellent music. He learns to play, usually in simplified form in the beginning, some of the great musical themes of all time. He usually learns some historical background about the composer and the country where that composer lived.

When a youngster knows good music, even though he may for a time find an interest in rock music, he won't forget good music. It cannot be taken away from him. To be honest, when I come home before I am expected, I don't know if I will find the local rock station or a classical piece blaring from our stereo system. More and more often I find the classical albums pulled out, and there seems to be less and less rock music.

Plan a wonderful evening out to take your kids to the symphony. Choose an evening when there is music they can enjoy. Modern symphony orchestras are becoming very creative. No more do you have to be put to sleep by three hours of soft chamber music. Now there are laser light shows to accompany the orchestra. There are whole evenings where themes from movies are the symphony's fare for the evening. For example, many orchestras perform the music from the *Star Wars* space trilogy.

If the Boston Pops orchestra ever comes to your area, do everything you can to hear them. They are absolutely delightful.

Find out as much as you can about the instruments so that you can point them out to the kids. When the tympani are booming, point that out. When the French horn utters its mellow call, show them where the French horn players are located. Talk before the symphony, during the intermission, and afterward about how these people have become excellent at what they do by consistent practice. Emphasize the value of sticking with something until it is accomplished.

See if you can take the kids backstage to meet the conductor or some of the musicians. It will make an indelible impression on them. Who knows? Perhaps there is a budding concert musician at your house.

In some cities concerts are held in local parks. Here in our city the symphony orchestra presents a series of summer concerts called Brownbag Concerts, which usually take place at noon in a downtown park. Everyone brings their lunch and listens.

We went once when the *1812 Overture* was being played. The *1812 Overture* is the piece that uses live cannons as part of the music. It was fun to watch them set off the big guns. Smoke poured from the barrel of the cannon, and the sound reverberated off the surrounding buildings. It was great fun to sit in the sunshine and listen to some really wonderful music being performed by a fine orchestra.

TRAVELING EXHIBITS   King Tut was only one of the many traveling exhibits we've seen over the last few years. It was one that made a great impression on all of us, but there have been other notable exhibits as well. Let me mention some of them.

Not too many years ago the local art museum had on display eggs which were handcrafted by the Fabergé family for the czar of Russia as gifts to family members. They are exquisite.

Some have little doors that open to tiny scenes. One has a huge emerald set at the top. Others have miniature scenes in complete detail painted all around the egg.

Another display at the local art museum was the gold of the Incas. We often think of the Incan culture as being very primitive, but a look at these golden treasures would convince you otherwise. Among the treasures was fabric of an intricate design that was shot through with golden threads.

Several times in the last few years the tall ships have made our city a port of call. It is spectacular to see these huge sailing vessels all rigged and moving out to sea.

During the bicentennial celebration a number of years ago, the Constitution of the United States made a tour across the country. Another time there was a full display of medieval armor, featuring pieces of armor used at different times in history. Currently in our city the Son of Heaven exhibit from China is on display. The display shows clay figures removed from a grave in China. Recently a working display of Chinese crafts was exhibited in our city. There was everything from papermaking to silk tapestry weaving on a gigantic ancient loom.

Universities and colleges often have traveling exhibits available to the public. It was at our local university that we saw some well-known Leonardo da Vinci paintings and sketches.

Watch your newspaper for information about these traveling exhibits. Call local museums, art galleries, and ticket offices to see what is being planned for your area.

DINNER OUT   Laurie, a business associate, tells a delightful story of the first time she and her husband, David, took their children to a very nice restaurant.

The children had received good report cards. In addition, their teachers had commended both of the children for their effort, and Laurie and David value hard work. They want their children to reach the level of their ability by working hard. So to show them how much they appreciated their efforts, they decided to take them to dinner.

They chose a local restaurant that uses cloth tablecloths and napkins and tall-stemmed glasses. Everyone in the family was dressed in their best clothes. It was a very special evening for this family, and one they treasure.

If it is at all possible to squeeze it into your budget, take your kids out to eat in nice places. Teach them which fork to use and when. Then later in their lives when they are confronted by an array of silver, they will not be intimidated and never will be ill at ease in a social situation where they are confronted by a long line of cutlery. You are giving them the skills they need to leave you, and among the skills they need to learn are social skills.

Eating out can be an ethnic adventure. We've eaten borsch in a Russian restaurant, true East Indian food which none of us liked, and, of course, Mexican food dozens of times. We've also wandered into English tea shops at high tea time. What a delightful experience!

Unfortunately my children were not along to share a cultural eating experience I had in a small cafe in New Orleans. It was like stepping backward in time about forty years. The posters on the walls were wartime issues as were the pictures. Behind the counter the owner was up to his elbows in hot water scrubbing glasses. As he washed, he visited with his customers who were lined up outside the door.

The food was so different from what I normally would eat for breakfast that, for me, that restaurant was a cultural experience. The next time I went to New Orleans I went back to experience it again.

Be bold and see what eating adventures you can discover. In doing so, you are exposing your children to a broader view of life, and are creating patterns of interest that will expand them as people. You, too, will grow as a person as you share these adventures with your children.

SPORTING EVENTS Almost every village and town in the nation has some kind of sporting event going on most of the year. In the fall it may be high school football; in winter, basketball; in spring, baseball. Larger cities have professional teams playing the same sports as well as hockey, soccer, and a host of others.

But other events are worth considering. A couple of years ago we took our kids to the national ice skating championships. We had watched some of the performers on television for years. What a thrill it was to see them zoom up to the end of the rink and look right up at us. What a joy to see the grace, the form, and the athletic prowess of the skaters.

After that it was easy to discuss with our kids having a vision in life and working to fulfill that goal, knowing full well that it may cost you dearly.

There are local swim meets to attend. Swim meets are noisy, fun events. There's the starting gun banging away, the splash as the participants hit the water, the water being flung from flying arms and feet, the touch, and the finish. Of course, they are even more fun when someone you know is participating.

A while back Wendy, Ed, and I had a fun time on a cross-country skiing trip. After we had skied we heard that a contest was being held by local people at a nearby ski bowl. We drove out and arrived at the same time as the contestants. One of the events was a ski-jumping contest. There were no chair lifts for the contestants. They had to climb up the hill, strap on their skis, and come roaring down the run, leaping into the air about midway on the ramp. We held our breath as one man, a veteran ski jumper, leaped into the air, fell flat on the snow, and slid fifty feet—on his stomach. He was all right, and got up laughing.

This was a spontaneous, serendipitous adventure that we took advantage of on the spot. Part of the adventure of family living is just that—being ready to take advantage of whatever opportunity presents itself.

CIRCUS Every few years take the kids to the circus if you possibly can. The circus is pure hype and fun. There is so much going on at a circus that you will enjoy watching your little ones' heads turn and their eyes light up with wonder.

A fun thing to do in conjunction with the circus is to go an hour or so before the performance and ask the circus personnel if you can walk through the area where the caged animals are kept. Sometimes you can get very close, and your little ones can get a good look at lions, tigers, and elephants. If you hang around long enough you may see the elephants dressed for their performance. There are all kinds of interesting people running around backstage at a circus. As I said, it is great fun.

A night on the town can be lots of fun for a family. Being together and sharing new adventures is probably the greatest value that can be derived from a night on the town. But once again, just being there with your children, talking about what you are doing and seeing, and sharing your life and your values with them is vitally important. Think about how you can have a night on the town with your kids.

11

One-on-One

"On my day we climbed Mount Si," Mark bragged to his sister.

"Well on my day we went roller skating, ate pizza, and played miniature golf," Wendy told him.

"My day" was a highlight of the children's year. They were always either looking forward or backward to it. It was a time near their birthdays when they spent an entire day with Dad, and could choose any activity their hearts desired. And Dad paid the bills.

Because we had only two children, when Dad took one for this special day, I was left with the other one. We made this a special time for us as well by doing something together, although not as expensive or as spectacular as what the birthday child was experiencing. Sometimes it was a good day to catch up on shopping for the non-birthday child.

We found this to be one of the most valuable investments we made in raising the kids. The time spent one-on-one—parent and child—was worth every dime it cost. Self-esteem blossomed as Dad took quality time to have fun with the child, to really listen without the competition that often comes from other siblings and even from another parent. It was a time for eyeballing the child and really finding out what was going on inside his head. It was a time from which a child could come away thinking, "Hey, I'm really important to Dad. Mom really does love me."

Statistics tell us that fathers today spend only minutes each week with their children. Pressure of jobs, commitments to civic and church activities, travel, and all that goes with it take their toll until, even if the father is at home in the evenings, he often does not have enough energy to communicate with his children.

Dates With Dad and Mom

One day a year will not solve the problems of fathers relating to their children, but it is one small step that can be taken to help the situation.

Ed "dated" the children until they left home. Sometimes I heard him say to Wendy, "Would you like to go to a Sonics game with me on Friday?" They would make a date for dinner and the game, and slip off to enjoy the evening together.

Mark and I still date. When Ed is out of town traveling we often go to dinner and a movie. It is something he enjoys greatly, and I enjoy being with him.

One evening not long ago we had dinner and wonderful conversation at a local restaurant. Mark told me about his goals, his plans for the future, and just the current stuff that was going on in his life. I had a chance to share some of what was happening in my life.

Then we drove to the theater. We had missed the first showing of the movie we wanted to see, so we decided to wait for the late showing. In the meantime we wandered around a shopping mall. We went to a computer store and looked at all the new games. Then we wandered by a yogurt shop. There in the shop sat a large number of young people from our church. Mark went in to talk with them, and I window-shopped at a nearby store.

When he came out he said, "Those guys wanted to know what I was doing out with my mother. I told them we were waiting to go to a movie. They said, 'You go out with your mother?' I told them that I sure do."

"How did that make you feel, Mark?" I asked.

"Ah, I don't care what they think."

With that, we went to the movie and had a wonderful time. It wasn't the last time either. We've had a number of nice evenings together since.

This special one-on-one time enables the parent to give focused attention to the child even if he is grown. It establishes warmth and understanding between them. In the informality of such times, the parent often is able to discern where the child's value system is headed. If we listen with our hearts to what our kids are saying, we will find they really want to communicate with those they consider the most important people to them on earth. Whether you believe it or not, those most important people are you, their parents. Kids hate the alienation that comes between them and their parents as much as parents do, but they lack experience in expressing their feelings and in knowing how to work through the alienation.

I talked recently with a woman whose post-teen son has been somewhat alienated from the family for several years. Just recently he and his mother have established a new relationship. They take walks together, and they spend long hours in the evenings sharing. The change has come about for several reasons. One is the process of maturation. The young man is feeling better about himself and is beginning to become an adult. The other big reason is that God has done a new work in his heart, and that, more than anything else, is affecting the way he feels about his parents.

Focused Attention

Dorothy Briggs, well-known writer and psychologist, says in her book *Your Child's Self-Esteem:* "Every child needs periodic genuine encounters with his parents. Genuine encounter is simply focused attention. It is attention with a special intensity born of direct, personal involvement. Vital contact means being intimately open to the particular, unique qualities of your child."[1]

In other words, every child needs some high-quality one-on-one time with each parent. This does not mean quantity time. If the parent is there in body only and scarcely hears what the child is saying to him, the child will pick up on that very quickly and will turn off the parent. In later years when the child becomes a teen, the parent will wonder why he doesn't want to talk, why he doesn't listen to the parent, and why he is sullen so much of the time. Guess why.

[1]Dorothy Corkille Briggs, *Your Child's Self-Esteem* (Garden City, New York: Doubleday and Company, Inc., 1970), p. 64.

Dorothy Briggs says, "Children are highly sensitive to the degree of focused attention they receive. . . .Focused attention—direct involvement—'allhereness'; it is a quality that gets love across. It nourishes self-respect at the roots because it says, 'I care.' "[2]

The opposite of focused attention is called distancing. Busy people tend to answer "uh huh" to a child's chattering without ever really hearing what the child is saying. Or we listen with half an ear. The conversation might go something like this:

"Ginny, how was school today?"

"It was great, Mom. You know my friend, Sally? Well, she brought a white mouse to school for show and tell."

"She did, huh? Don't talk with your mouth full and please use your napkin. You have something running out of the corner of your mouth."

"And the mouse got loose in the classroom and—"

"Ginny, watch out! You're going to spill your milk."

At this point Ginny stops talking, grows silent, and dutifully watches her milk, her napkin, and her manners. Mom really didn't want to know about school. Mom really doesn't care, she thinks.

And Mom thinks she has just performed as a good mother, trying to guide her young daughter toward appropriate manners and excellent table decorum, but she's missed the opportunity to have an encounter of importance with her child.

I understand how that child feels. I know a man who always asked questions as if he were interested in what my answers might be, but before I could open my mouth to answer the question, he was on to something else. I wanted to shout at him, "Why do you ask me questions if you don't care what I have to say?" I realized that in his line of work he was supposed to be interested in people and had trained himself to ask the right questions, but he had not learned to focus his attention on the person.

When I was but a college student, I met a woman whose husband held an influential position in the denomination of which I am a part. I was a nobody from the sticks of Montana, but when this woman asked me a question, she riveted her

[2]Ibid., p. 65.

eyes on mine. Even though we were in a huge crowd which enveloped us on both sides, she never took her eyes from my face. I never have forgotten that woman. I felt like somebody important when I was with her. It is no wonder to me that she is deeply loved wherever she goes.

That's the difference between focused attention and distancing. One person had the ability to make me feel important and loved, and the other made me feel inferior and stupid. And that's the way it is with our children. They need us to be there for them, listening, interested, concerned, caring. It takes so little time to convey that feeling. I talked only ten minutes with this woman more than twenty-five years ago, but I've never forgotten the encounter.

As I write this, I wish I could say I always focused my attention on my own children. I didn't, and I don't, and they tell me so periodically.

"Mom, you're not listening."

"Yes I am."

"No you're not. Put that down and listen. I want to tell you something important."

And I realize they are right. I really wasn't listening at all. That's the reason I know what the table conversation in our earlier story was like. I well could have been that mother—too busy, in too much of a hurry, too much of the time.

But the kids and I did have times of focused attention periodically, and we did build an excellent friendship. Many times when Wendy was a teenager the bedroom door would open late at night and she'd say, "Mom, is Dad traveling?" If the answer was yes she would come in and sprawl on the bed, and we would talk until two or three in the morning. If the answer was no she'd say, "Can you come out and talk for a while?" I'd climb out of bed even if I had been asleep, pull on my robe, and we'd go to the kitchen for something warm to drink while we talked and talked.

Focus on the Child

It's easy to focus so intently on doing things for the child that we forget to focus on the child himself. Ed said that during the period he was reading Dorothy Briggs's material on focused attention, he went out to throw a Frisbee with Mark. Suddenly he heard himself saying, "No Mark, that's not the way to do it. Hurry up, throw it!" and so on. Instead of focusing on the playtime or on the child, Ed was focusing on Mark's getting it right, doing it Ed's way, and hurrying so Ed could have fun. He caught himself, stopped nagging, and made a conscious effort to focus on the person Mark is.

In addressing how much encounter a child needs, Dorothy says, "How often do children need encounter? The more, the better, but constant encounter is unnecessary. We don't ordinarily feel unloved when we lack exclusive attention. It is when others *never* have time to be truly with us that we feel unimportant. If children feel your wholehearted presence periodically, they can tolerate times when your attention is elsewhere."[3]

Each summer for many years, Ed and Mark planned a special focused attention encounter time—a two- or three-day camping trip. They spent days deciding what food to take and then purchasing it. Then they packed their gear and headed for the hills. One trip they both reminisce about so much was to a place called Deer Park near Hurricane Ridge in Olympic National Park.

They set up their tent on a big ridge with a tremendous view of the valley, snowcapped mountains, and hills covered with flowers. The first night out, Ed started to cook dinner for Mark, who then was eight years old. We recently had purchased a new camping stove. Ed tried and tried to attach a hose from the propane bottle to the stove, but just couldn't do it. Mark told him several times, "Dad, why don't you turn the hose around?"

"Leave me alone, Mark. I know what I'm doing," Ed retorted. After he had struggled for ten or fifteen minutes, a park ranger came along and asked, "Can I help you? Are you having trouble?"

"I just can't seem to get this thing on," Ed told him.

The ranger took the hose, looked at it, then said, "Oh, let's just turn it around."

[3]Ibid., p. 69.

At that, Ed shot Mark a don't-you-dare-say-anything look.

This trip had been planned to coincide with the annual Perseids meteor shower that occurs the second week in August. The best time to see the meteor shower is after midnight. After dinner they slept for a while, and at about 11:30 P.M. they walked to a hillside to watch for meteors. Imagine their surprise when they found several other people on the hillside with them. A meteor shower may not be as exciting as it sounds. It does not mean the sky is filled with streaking meteors. Usually you see one about every ten or fifteen minutes. So after about an hour of sitting in the cool mountain air, they returned to their campsite, only to find that a mouse had moved into their tent. They spent a few minutes chasing it out, and then at last settled down for the night.

The next day they met an old man they called Gramps. He had been coming to Deer Park for years, and was very knowledgeable about the area's flora and fauna. He showed them two plants which are endemic to the area, which means that they grow there and nowhere else.

Later in the day when they were hiking, they came upon a clump of small evergreens, peered into the brush, and had another special treat. There curled up sleeping was a young deer.

During that one trip Ed and Mark built dozens of memories that only they share. They came back acting like two thieves who just had stumbled upon a treasure. You could tell something wonderful had happened, but Wendy and I just couldn't quite grasp how wonderful it had been for the two of them.

The Stuff Life Is Made Of

When Prince Charles married Diana the archbishop looked at them and said, "This is the stuff fairy tales are made of." In contrast, parenting one-on-one is *not* the stuff fairy tales are made of. It is the stuff relationships are made of; it is the stuff trust is made of; it is the stuff memories are made of. Sometimes it is the stuff which prevents a lot of negative stuff from happening.

One day when Mark was in the seventh grade I happened to come home from work a little early, about the time he should have arrived from school. He didn't come and he didn't come. I waited and tried not to worry about him.

After a while he came home. "Where have you been, Mark? You know the rule is you come home right after school, and then if you want to go someplace you check with me first."

"I've been at the Seven-Eleven."

"What have you been doing there?"

"Playing video games."

"Mark, I don't want you hanging around there playing video games. I want you to come home right after school. Do you understand?"

"I hear you, but I don't understand what's so bad about playing video games."

"It isn't the video games; it's the loitering around a convenience store. You know that is one of the places drugs are sold."

"Yeah, but I'm not going to do drugs."

"Nevertheless, you come home."

A few weeks later it happened again. This time, Mark was punished, but in addition to that, we began to think about a possible solution to the problem. Mark really was not interested in hanging around the convenience store. He really *did* want to play video games.

So I asked Ed, "Do you think you could take Mark to the video parlor and play games with him occasionally? I could do it, but I'm so terrible at it that I don't think it would be much fun for either one of us."

"Sure," Ed replied, "that would be fun."

So once a week Ed filled his pocket with quarters, and he and Mark slipped off to play video games. Later on a young man came into our lives who became like our own son. He was the best at playing video games. He could make a quarter last until he was too worn out to play the game. His name always topped the list of the high scorers. Many nights he joined Ed and Mark, and they had a wonderful time playing games.

That ended the problem of loitering after school at the local convenience store. Mark so looked forward to playing games with his dad and our friend that he gave up hanging around with his own friends after school. It wasn't always convenient for Ed to lay aside his plans for the evening and go play games with Mark. Sometimes he simply got sick of going to the video parlor again and again, but he did it because it was important to Mark.

Pay Attention Now

The time to invest time in your children is when they need it. It doesn't pay to save for their college education if that means scrimping on the activities that would buy relationships with them. It doesn't pay to delay spending time with them for so long that one day they would rather be with their friends than with you. The time to act in relationship building with your kids is right *now*.

One-on-one time begins when your children are tiny babies. It begins during those first few weeks when you look right into their tiny faces and talk to them. It continues when the toddler drags a doll across the floor and says, "Dadda, play house," and you're paying the bills. It's there when a three-year-old child says, "Rock me," and you're right in the middle of making a cake.

I'm not saying children's wants should rule our schedules. I'm not saying we should drop everything whenever a youngster wants to play. Children must learn give and take too. But we need to evaluate their request for our time. What is the need behind this request? Does the whiny three-year-old child need to be rocked because he is feeling insecure? Is the toddler trying to say, "Pay attention to me, I'm important too"? Those moments when our children need us become further and further apart as they grow older. We can't afford to waste these moments when our children are young simply because we're too busy.

A few hours or a few days of focused attention on a child pays off in huge dividends. Maybe for a little while we could stop being the perfect parents and just enjoy the little people God has given us. Very soon they will grow into big people, move away, and have lives of their own.

As you focus your attention one-on-one with your children, you will discover that you are living with some delightful people. When you stop looking at their faults and imperfections you'll discover they have hundreds of wonderful qualities. Don't let their teachers, friends, or the parents of their friends be the ones to discover how neat your kids are. Take some time and find it out for yourself.

12

The Ultimate Adventure

The Maid of the Mist tour boat churned up to the thundering wall of water. Niagara Falls is impressive at any distance, but from this vantage point it was positively frightening.

"Kind of makes you know what the children of Israel felt like when they walked through the Red Sea, doesn't it?" Wendy yelled over the roar of the falls. I nodded a yes.

"We really look funny," I yelled back. And we did look funny wearing long black raincoats that only partially shielded us from the water. Our sopping hair hung around our faces. With their short hair, the guys were faring a little better. At least it wasn't hanging in their faces.

The trip to Niagara Falls was part of an extended driving vacation to New England. We were having fun even if we were drowning. When the boat landed at the dock, standing there waiting to board was the well-known singer Wayne Newton. I walked right by him, and wondered who the guy was with all the rings. The kids were thrilled.

An annual vacation of some kind was and is an absolute necessity for our busy family. Both Ed and I deal with a lot of people all the time in our jobs. It is essential that we get away from responsibilities, telephones, and schedules sometime during the year.

The truth is that every family needs a vacation. It's a wonderful time to spend together as a family. It's a great time for getting to know our kids better, for finding out what is going on in their heads, and for teaching values. There are plenty of opportunities during a two- to three-week vacation for teaching values.

It also can be a time of great stress for some families. Most families are not used to being shut up together in a car for hours on end. Someone once said, "There are two ways to travel—first class and with kids." Spending twenty-four hours a day with your kids is very different, especially for dads, from the usual routine—a quick bedtime story, a prayer, and a good-night kiss.

Some of the stress related to vacationing can be avoided by advance thinking and planning. One thing we can do is to *reduce expectations of what the vacation should be*. We need to learn to relax and just take it as it comes. Who says we have to make 700 miles a day? This is supposed to be a vacation, and believe it or not, getting there can be half the fun if we slow down and enjoy it.

Overachieving, active people probably tend to plan too much into their vacations. It is something our family has to guard against because none of us likes to sit still for very long. For example, our trip to New England was too far for the time we had. But we are fast learners, and we never again will try to drive across the continent and back in three weeks.

Planning ahead can help to reduce stress. Nothing is worse than a car of tired, hungry, cranky kids (and spouses) who have nowhere to spend the night. Have you ever pulled into a town late at night and found the annual rodeo has filled every bed for miles? We did. There's nothing to do but hit the road and keep driving until you find someplace to stay. And in Montana, that could be a hundred or more miles.

Continually spending more money than you had planned greatly increases stress. Vacationing isn't much fun for the bill payer when that person realizes what is going to happen once the family returns home. Seriously consider discovering some free things you can do along the way. Some planning, such as writing to travel bureaus, will help you to locate those places that offer free activities.

Another stress reducer is to think about what the family can do in the car while driving from one place to another. I have offered a number of practical suggestions elsewhere in this book. Think about the journey from a child's perspective. What would you want to do if you were shut up tightly with brothers and sisters in an eight-by-five-foot enclosure? You would want to tease and pick on them until they were fighting mad, just to have something to do. I remember the feeling from my own childhood. I'd be so bored I wanted to scream. So I'd start picking on my two brothers. I'd try to see how much ruckus I could cause without getting into trouble myself. Woe be to us if Dad slowed the car and started to pull to the side of the road. That meant big trouble for all of us.

Take frequent breaks on driving vacations. We found that everything went better for us if we avoided restaurants (more sitting) and ate at least some of our meals in a park or even at a roadside rest area. A fast, hard game of tag or Frisbee helps to get rid of a lot of pent-up energy. Let the kids run off their energy to their hearts' content.

Recognize that problems will occur. Problems abound when you are traveling. There can be car problems, kids can get sick in cars, motel reservations can get twisted up, and the attractions you wanted to see can cost too much. Try to stay flexible and see what creative solutions you can find to solve those problems. Who knows? You may come up with a better idea than the original plan. Your children will learn about problem solving as they watch you cope with problems on your family's vacation trip.

An interesting trend is happening in America today with regard to family vacations. The two-week family vacation is losing popularity and the weekend vacation is on the increase. The family is not traveling as far; 300 to 500 miles is about average.

Maybe it is a good trend. Perhaps families would relax and enjoy each other more if they spent less time in the car and more time playing. Whatever the trend, it is important to take time to rest and play. The Bible teaches the idea of Sabbath rest. God worked six days, and then He ended His work and rested. God's plan in the Old Testament was for the land to lie fallow every seven years to give it a rest.

Rest is God's idea, and it is a good idea. We must fight to maintain rest in a culture that becomes increasingly busy every year. Take a vacation, play with your kids, and be renewed in your mind and strength. Only you can decide if a number of mini-vacations will give you the rest you need, or if you will need a two- or even a three-week vacation to rest.

Consider the ages of your children when planning your vacation. Small children are just as happy with a short trip to a beach or lake as they would be to a great attraction like Walt Disney World.

Don't be afraid to travel with very young children. Recently I witnessed some truly creative mothering at O'Hare International Airport in Chicago. A very young mother was seated cross-legged on the floor. Near her a large bag was open at the top. From this she handed food to a bouncing toddler. Lying on a folded blanket on the floor in front of her was a four-month-old infant.

Suddenly I realized the air around them was filled with bubbles. She was blowing soap bubbles to the delight of her two youngsters. We, the rest of the passengers in the waiting area, watched with interest as the baby kicked and cooed and followed the bubbles with his eyes. The toddler was bouncing around and trying to burst as many of the bubbles as possible. This clever, young mother turned what could have been a tiring and difficult situation into a time of sharing and joy.

Traveling with young children does demand creativity on the parents' part. It also demands that we keep everything simple. The advantage to starting with simple family vacations is that as time goes on, you can make them increasingly more appealing to growing kids and finally to teenagers merely by planning bigger and better events. I don't know too many teenagers who would turn down a chance to go to Hawaii. Our adult children still arrange their schedules to be with us on a vacation if the stakes are high enough. Last summer Wendy spent ten days with us in England.

Theme Vacations

One of the things we enjoyed during the years our children were at home was to take theme vacations. These were vacations in which we planned as many events as we could find around a single idea.

The first of these was a trip to Disneyland. This was not only a trip to a great amusement park, but also an opportunity to learn about some great children's literature since so many of the park's attractions are based on children's books.

By doing a little research, I discovered that one of the rides is based on *The Wind in the Willows* by Kenneth Grahame. Another ride, the spinning teacups, is based on *Alice in Wonderland*. On another we boarded a Treasure Island pirate ship. Sleeping Beauty's Castle is a focal point of both Disneyland and Walt Disney World. A giant tree house depicts the home in *Swiss Family Robinson*.

We either had read all of these stories before we arrived in Anaheim, or we read them on the way. When we took Mr. Toad's wild ride which ended with the illusion of a train about to run over us, we knew the story behind the ride. Through reading, we already had visualized walking the beaches with Swiss Family Robinson as they looked for turtle eggs to eat. In our minds we had helped them haul lumber up the giant tree to make their home. It was great fun to climb up to their tree house in Disneyland and remember what we had read.

In 1977 we took a Bicentennial tour. The Bicentennial was celebrated in 1976, but we couldn't afford the trip that year. Besides, we thought Washington, D.C., would be so packed with tourists we wouldn't be able to see much, so we waited. It was a good decision.

In order for us to take this theme vacation, we had to be very careful with our finances. Early in the planning stages Ed arranged for us to stay in an apartment complex in Alexandria, Virginia. It had a kitchen, which meant we could cook our own meals and save a lot of money. It was also on a major bus line, which meant we could leave our car parked, and reduce both our stress and the amount of money we spent.

We had enough relatives across the country that we could drive from one place to the next without having to rent a motel room. They were glad to see us, and staying with them also helped with finances.

Another money saver was cooking our own meals en route at roadside rest areas and parks. An ice chest in the trunk and a small folding camp stove with a propane bottle, plus half a dozen cooking implements, paper plates, and plastic eating utensils were all we needed. The cooking was mostly one-dish suppers with fruit or a green salad and cookies to complete the meal. In about thirty minutes we could fix dinner, clean up, and be on our way.

Because breakfast is an inexpensive meal and the kids didn't need to run off energy that early in the day, we usually ate breakfast in restaurants.

Allow some flexibility in your schedule for meals, whether you eat outdoors or in restaurants. Be prepared to change your plans if needed. On one of our trips across the country we had an experience eating outdoors that convinced us we couldn't be too rigid about cooking our own meals to save money.

We stopped at a site in eastern Montana, set up the camp stove and food, and began cooking. The sky had been threatening rain for hours, but we thought we could outrun the storm. We set up in a picnic shelter just in case the storm caught up with us. Dinner was very enjoyable, except for the approaching black clouds. When I started to wash the dishes, the storm hit. Hailstones as big as golf balls bounced off the roof of the shelter, the wind forced the rain in through the sides, and an umbrella and plastic tablecloth didn't do much to protect us from its fury. Rain poured down for ten or fifteen minutes, and we grew colder by the minute.

It was a sodden group who checked into a motel later that evening. When we flipped on the news we heard a tornado had been sighted in the exact location of that roadside rest stop at the exact time we were there. We didn't know whether to laugh or cry.

The next night when the sky again threatened to unleash torrents of rain, we decided not to risk it and ate in a very warm, dry restaurant.

In Washington, D.C., we had breakfast at the apartment we had rented, and then I made lunch and tucked it in my large purse. We waited to have dinner until we returned to the apartment in the evenings. There I cooked a full meal just like at home. I never will forget having my purse checked as we went through security at the White House. The attendant looked inside and said, "Hmmm, lunch." Then he winked and cleared me to enter. Brown-bagging it in the city parks put us right in there with government workers who do the same.

To enhance the theme idea, all the way from Washington State to Washington, D.C., we read books about the Revolutionary War period of our country's history and about the founding and settling of the areas we passed. I found many excellent pre-teen books on the subject. One book, about a family which operated a flour mill, described the millstone and how the grooves had to be sharpened to grind the corn. Later in our trip we came upon a millstone. As we ran our hands over the notched grooves, the story had new meaning for us.

We had prearranged tours of the Senate, the House of Representatives, and the White House. These can be arranged with your congressmen and senators. We spent a couple of days touring the Smithsonian Institution; then we went to Arlington Cemetery for the changing of the guard. We also went to all the monuments, including the top of the Washington Monument.

One evening we drove down the Potomac to Mount Vernon for a sound and light show. Here we sat in one of the most historic places in the country, the home of our first president, and our kids were most interested in a praying mantis they discovered on the top of a post. They spent more than half an hour watching this bug. It wasn't what Ed and I had intended they get out of the evening, but it didn't matter. If you ask them today about Mount Vernon, they will talk about that praying mantis.

After seeing Washington, D.C., we drove down to Williamsburg, Virginia. We spent two wonderful days stepping back in history to the time of our forefathers. We ate in a pub where George Washington used to gather with his friends. The visit gave all of us a base for understanding the gentility of the early English settlers of our country. We came away from the entire trip with a better understanding of our government and history, and valuing more than ever the fact we were born in America.

A third theme vacation really turned into a theme summer. Almost everything we did that summer was related to Native Americans. We camped on the Washington coast near an Indian village, and then hiked seven miles to an archeological dig where university students were unearthing an ancient Indian village. It was fascinating to see the layout of the buildings and to realize that a very prosperous village once had hummed with life in this place.

Then it was on to Neah Bay to see the Makah Indian Museum. A few weeks later we saw a play called *This is Your Land* which was about the settling of the Northwest. It, too, had much information about the Indian culture and the relationship between the settlers and Indians.

We toured Fort Vancouver in Vancouver, Washington, one of the first settlements on the West Coast where Indians and settlers mixed. And to round out the summer, we went canoeing on Lake Washington.

Theme vacations can be fun. The experiences build one upon another to make a complete learning circle. There are many more theme vacation ideas which are just waiting for you to discover. Try to pull as many learning experiences as possible, related to one idea, into your vacation. It can be plays, books you read, exhibits you visit, people you talk to, museums you tour, and foods you eat. (We didn't do this, but it would have been fun to eat an authentic Indian meal.)

Consider what your area offers. Is it the Amish culture? Can you make a theme vacation of visiting their area? Is it traveling via flatboat or riverboat on this country's major waterways? Can you follow a theme about that subject? Could you tour plantations? Is there enough information and places to see to make it a theme vacation? Is there a Spanish influence? Can you follow that trail? Is your area renowned for its beauty? Could your theme follow from one beautiful spot to the next?

I don't have the answers to these questions. It is up to you to find them. In finding the answers you are opening the doorway to some exciting adventures for your family. And what is the value of these adventures? Ask your children's teachers about the value of seeing something firsthand. Ask them how it will enhance your children's education. Nothing can take the place of seeing it for yourself, of seeing where history was made.

You can ask our kids about how wool was spun and dyed, wood shingles were shaped, and boots were made in colonial times. They know because they've seen it demonstrated firsthand. These and hundreds more firsthand experiences were gleaned from family theme vacations.

Family History Vacations

Another kind of vacation is the family history vacation. Every family has roots somewhere. It is great fun and very informative to trace your family's roots and to visit the places where your family began in this country.

We did this three times. The first time was part of the Bicentennial trip. When Ed was a boy he had moved from New Jersey to California. He never had been back to New Jersey. So we decided to visit his hometown and neighborhood.

We found the house where he had spent the first twelve years of his life. He told our children how the house had been moved to make room for a freeway. He took them down to the lot where he had played as a boy and he marvelled at how someone had shrunken the entire neighborhood. Nothing was as big as he remembered it.

A second family history vacation took us to the Pike's Peak region of Colorado. Our children's maternal great-grandfather's name had been Pike before he was adopted by another family. He had been related to Zebulon Pike, the great explorer of the Rocky Mountain area.

We put up our tent in the shadow of the mountain named for our children's ancestor. It was a wonderful time. We also read some books about the settling of that territory by early explorers, trappers, and mountain men.

Another part of that family history vacation was a side trip to Cripple Creek, Colorado, where my grandfather had worked in the gold mines to feed and clothe his family. My father had told me about the wild burros he and his brother used to chase. There are still lots of burros around Cripple Creek. We imagined him as a boy wandering up and down these streets. We tried to decide where the ice cream shop had been. According to my father, the owner of the shop always set nearly empty ice cream cans outside just as school was ending for the day. All the kids carried spoons in their back pockets. The local kids made the shop a regular stop on the way home from school.

Then we went to Victor, Colorado, where Dad and his brother had rolled a huge truck tire down a hill and almost smashed their own house, and we saw the grade school where he had fallen off the fire escape and broken his jaw.

All of the stories which my father had told our kids suddenly came alive and took on new meaning when they were standing on the same soil he had lived and walked on as a boy.

What are your family's origins? Could you pursue a family history vacation? Such a vacation gives continuity to your family. It gives your kids a sense of belonging to something that has gone on for a long time. It traces your heritage and anchors your kids in terms of knowing where they fit into the family.

Camping Vacations

We took many camping vacations with the kids. We all like the outdoors, but that isn't the primary reason we camped. For us, camping was a means to an end. If we had waited until we could have afforded to stay in hotel accommodations, we never would have gone anyplace. We all wanted to go and so we camped.

Tent-camping vacations put you in some of the most beautiful places in America. We've camped in Yellowstone, Glacier, Olympic, and Mt. Rainier national parks. We've camped in the mountains of California and at Niagara Falls—and a lot of places in between.

This kind of camping has its challenges. One night it rained so hard in Yosemite National Park all the garbage cans in the campground were floating, and we stepped barefoot out of the tent into a foot of ice water.

You meet some interesting creatures when you are camping. Once in Utah's desert overfriendly ground squirrels and lizards wanted to come in through the screening of our tent. Another time we heard something slipping and sliding down the roof of the tent, scrambling up, and then sliding down again. We suspect the acrobatic culprits were chipmunks.

But most of the time camping in a tent is not too hard. We're not the rugged type of campers who set up camp twenty miles from everyone else. We always tried to camp in state parks with hot showers and that all-important commodity for teenagers—outlets for their electric hair dryers. Some of the campsites themselves have electricity. I guess you could bring a microwave and hook it up if you desired.

Most campgrounds have a grocery store on the grounds or nearby. Some have video games. Many have places to swim, and almost all have evening campfire programs and other park-ranger-directed activities, like nature walks, contests (slug racing or whatever), and demonstrations. So you see, it's not so tough. Add to that the beautiful sights, and camping is a very pleasant experience.

I'll never forget the morning in Pike's Forest when Wendy and I got up early to go see if there were deer in the meadow. We passed by a camping trailer and saw a lady standing outside in her pajamas. The air around her head was filled with flying hummingbirds. She was taking down hummingbird feeders and filling them one by one. We heard her say, "Ouch, don't poke my hand," and we saw a hummingbird fly into the saucepan of red liquid. She turned and saw us and said, "I'll never let these feeders run out of food again. They've been flying at the trailer for hours. We can't sleep." Camping often offers some fresh surprises. I'm so glad Wendy and I have the hummingbird experience to share and to treasure.

"But you have to sleep on the ground when you camp," you might protest. Yes, that's true, and I have to say that getting up gets a little harder every year. It is a long way up from the ground. But we slept on the ground on two inches of foam rubber or on four-inch-thick air mattresses. We had two tents during the years the children were at home. One was a nine-by-twelve cabin tent, and the other was a four-man backpacking tent. We alternated according to need. In both we were extremely comfortable.

It is a wonderful feeling for a family to bed down in a small tent and have someone say, "Mom, Dad, tell us about when you were little." Then we lay there and told stories, accompanied by the wind sighing in the trees, until one by one, the listeners drifted off to sleep.

We like tent camping because it is so simple. Everything can be tucked into the trunk of a car or at least into the trunk and a car-top carrier. It is necessary to resist the temptation to pack everything, including the kitchen sink.

Although we chose tent camping, there are other ways to camp that may be a little more comfortable for some families. One time we were sitting at a campsite in a state park when the longest, biggest motor home I've ever seen pulled in and tried to maneuver down the narrow, winding roads of the campsite. We looked at each other and said, "There's living proof you *can* take it with you."

For many years my brother had a folding tent trailer. It was a very functional unit in which his family was very comfortable. He did not mind pulling a trailer behind his car, and so for them it worked well.

Our equipment list for camping included the following:

1. tent—our backpacking tent weighs only ten pounds
2. sleeping bags and either air mattresses or foam pads
3. small pillows—I made some with handles which also work on airplanes
4. camp stove—ours folds to the size of a briefcase and uses bottled propane
5. nesting pots and pans to conserve space
6. one Teflon-coated fry pan (for easy cleanup)
7. two enamel dishpans to sit on the camp stove for heating water for dishes, etc.
8. one pancake turner
9. one large spoon
10. one long sharp knife
11. locking pliers which are useful for many things, including taking hot cooking pots off the stove or campfire
12. can opener
13. folding water container which holds five gallons
14. matches
15. a small bottle of detergent
16. a pot scrubber
17. tablecloth
18. paper towels
19. paper plates
20. propane lantern and propane canister
21. plastic knives, forks, and spoons
22. thermal cups

All of this equipment could be nested together, and it all fit in one small box.

Unless we were going to some extremely hot location in the

middle of summer, everyone was required to take along a wool sweater and a raincoat of some kind. Evenings can be cool in many camping locations, and a wool sweater is good insurance.

In addition, we had a large ice chest for food. This had everything we needed in it, from breakfast cereal to meat for dinner. We didn't store a lot of perishable foods from day to day. We usually stopped somewhere in the morning and bought ice if we needed it and meat for supper. A trip to the supermarket was a welcome break either from traveling or from being in the woods.

Before leaving home we removed all staple items (like pasta mixes) from their boxes and repackaged them with the directions for cooking in lock-top plastic bags. It is amazing how much food you can put in one place if you get rid of the fancy packaging. When repackaging food for your family, remember everyone eats more outdoors. Use larger quantities than you normally would.

Breakfast was a simple affair with orange juice, cereal, peanut butter sandwiches, pancakes, or French toast. At all of our meals we tried to eat much the way we did at home. It avoided upset tempers and upset stomachs.

Breakfast cleanup and fixing lunch followed immediately after breakfast. Sandwiches for lunch were tucked away where they could be retrieved easily. Sandwiches, fruit, and cookies were the norm. We usually bought something to drink, and eating this light always left room for an afternoon snack.

The evening meal was also simple. We had some kind of meat, potatoes or pasta, a vegetable (usually canned), and fruit. I finally did get a bake oven which sits on the top of the camp stove. I have made pizza, biscuits, and even a cake in the oven. But the bake oven isn't a necessity.

Several weeks before the trip we would have a good idea of how many days we'd be cooking our own dinners, and at that time I'd plan all menus. Then I'd shop for food over the next few weeks, always watching for bargains.

Camping is a wonderful way to save money. However, it was never our intent to be so tight with money that no one had a good time. It was just that we wanted to spend our money for activities and adventures we wanted to do, like horseback rides around Lake Louise in Canada, taking the aerial tramway to the top of Whistlers' Mountain, seeing extra attractions at Disney-land, or seeing an extra play.

Family vacations can build wonderful memories. They are well worth the effort, time, and money invested in them to make them work well. They are rich times of sharing yourself, your values, and your love for your kids.

Approach the family vacation with great anticipation and expectation that this is going to be a great time for all of you. Plan ahead carefully—and have a great time together!

13

Europe at Last

"Oh, Mom, look," Wendy said excitedly as she peered out the window of the 747. "Look at all the red tile roofs in winding rows."

I don't know how I could have looked. Her head was blocking the window, and besides that I was airsick. But I was glad she was excited. We were about to land at Schipol International Airport in Amsterdam. Our dream was coming true. We actually had been able to put together enough money and enough time to take our kids to Europe.

I thought back to the day when we first had talked about this trip. What an impossible dream it had seemed that day. But God in His goodness had helped us find a way to make this dream come true, and God in His goodness can help you make your dreams come true too.

In a few minutes the plane rolled up to the terminal, and we weary passengers got off and started through customs. Each family member carried his own passport. We wanted them to fully experience every part of international travel, so each one went through customs on his or her own. We were stunned to see armed guards throughout the airport. We realized instantly we were not at home.

When we cleared customs a very close college friend of mine was waiting to whisk us off to her snug Dutch-styled home. She and her husband had been missionaries here for a number of years and were well adjusted to life in The Netherlands. And so our adventure began.

Why We Went to Europe

We had been dreaming about this trip for years, and one of our purposes was to see if we could fulfill that dream. As I said earlier in the book, we didn't make the kind of money it takes to go on a European trip.

About a year before we made the trip I said to Ed one day, "You know, if we are going to take these kids to Europe, we need to do it in the next year. Wendy is a junior in high school and Mark is in the seventh grade. She's going to be leaving us for college soon, and both of their schedules are going to become increasingly more complicated. I think this is the time to do it."

He looked at me and said, "Well, you know we don't have the money. The only thing I can think of is for you to get a job, and we'll save that money for the trip."

I had been free-lance writing for years, but it paid almost nothing. Although I had been writing rather consistently at home, I had been basically a housewife and full-time mother.

"I don't know what I can do. I don't know who would pay me to do what I know how to do. I don't know where to start. I think I'll just pray about it," I told Ed.

"You have to let people know you are looking for work," he encouraged.

"I don't even know how to do that, so I'm not going to tell anyone. I'm just going to pray."

"Nobody gets a job that way," he told me.

"Well it's the way I'm going to get one." I began to pray.

About two weeks later, a small publishing house in our area asked me to come in for an interview. I went somewhat reluctantly. I still wasn't sure I wanted to go back to work. I really had enjoyed being a full-time homemaker. So dragging my feet all the way, I went for the interview.

I laid down many conditions and barriers to their hiring me—but they did anyway. Soon I was working four days a week, eight hours a day, and loving it. We made the decision that we would not spend one penny of my earnings for a year. We would buy nothing we did not absolutely need, and maybe we wouldn't even buy things we needed. We would postpone any purchases for as long as possible.

And so we began saving and watching our little fund grow. When spring came and it was time to buy our tickets, it still looked very close, so close that we wondered if we dared order the airline tickets. With careful thinking and planning, we were able to figure out a way to make it all happen.

Our children watched this process, and I suppose held their breath wondering if the trip honestly was going to happen. They learned the value of saving money to accomplish a big goal. They also learned that you can't have everything you want along the way, and still have the money to do the truly important things. Choices have to be made. All the little choices not to spend money for frivolous things soon add up to the ability to do something big—in this case to take the trip.

On a grand scale, once again they learned that experiences are more important than things, and sometimes you have to sacrifice things to buy experiences. It is a lesson that we think they have learned well.

Recently we were talking with Mark about the rather beat-up car he is driving. "Don't you want to get a new car or at least a newer one?" we asked him.

"No," he told us, "I'd rather go back to Europe and make the old car do."

As I write these words, he is somewhere over the Atlantic Ocean returning from a Christmas trip to Europe. He paid for this experience entirely by himself, and he will drive the old car another year or two.

Another reason we wanted so much to take the kids to Europe was that we consider ourselves world Christians, and we wanted them to become world Christians, too. We wanted them to see other people in other places, and to be concerned about those people. We wanted them to have a broader view of life and Christianity than what they could experience here in the States.

We also wanted our children to be unafraid to travel to new places on their own. We wanted them to be free of fear so they can answer God's call to any corner of the globe. We wanted them to realize people are people wherever they live, and that all of us all over the earth are much the same, with the same hopes, ambitions, needs, wants, joys, and sorrows.

These goals for the trip have been and are being accomplished in both of their lives. Wendy has decided to spend her life in Europe helping troubled kids. She is there now on a short-term missionary assignment. She is unafraid to explore and experience this new culture—to go anywhere or do anything. After a time, she will come home and begin to prepare herself for a lifetime of living and working, probably in the inner cities of Europe. Of course, her plans are tentative, pending the will of God and His intervention in her life. She truly has become a world Christian.

Mark's goals are a little different and very much in the idea stage. He thinks he would like to work in international banking, and hopes that somehow his work also will be tied to missionary involvement. He hopes to live in Europe as well.

Another reason for taking the kids to Europe was so that we could be there to introduce them to the new cultures ourselves. Many kids travel abroad on their own in their late teens and early twenties, but we wanted to see how they reacted to each new situation—like the lunch of tongue we ate at the Swiss sidewalk cafe, and the meal in a restaurant where the customers' dogs were sitting on chairs at the table. I guess we were a little selfish in wanting to be with our two children as they discovered each new experience along with us. Ed and I had spent a number of weeks in Spain a few years earlier. We had not, however, been to the countries we now were visiting. This was an impossible dream coming true for Ed and me, too.

By being together we not only saw their reactions to new cultures and people, but they also saw ours. They could see we value people—no matter where they live in the world.

One of my favorite memories of France is Wendy talking to an old woman in French about the medieval cathedral in her city. The woman was very proud of its heritage, and wanted to tell us all about it. She was also pleased to find a young woman trying very hard to communicate in French. It was a delightful moment there on the street of that small town.

How We Did It

Planning was an absolute necessity. We planned to take our backpacking tent and a few camping items. The rest we could borrow from our friends in The Netherlands.

By having a tent along we could be much more flexible. Because almost every village and city in Europe has a wonderfully efficient camping facility nearby, we could count on staying there. Therefore we did not need to make hotel reservations, so we did not have to be anyplace at a certain time.

We rented a car from an agency in Denmark. We picked it up in Amsterdam and returned it to Brussels, thus avoiding a certain kind of tax that one must pay if picking up a car and returning it to the same location.

The car was equipped with four sleeping bags, four air mattresses, and four liners, so we didn't have to haul those from home. Since it cost only a pittance to stay in a campground, we also saved a lot of money.

We purchased our food along the way. It was always an adventure to find the local market and wander through looking for good things to eat. In fact, that pursuit became one of our favorites. When shopping in Europe or other foreign locations, remember to take along a basket or a string bag because very few markets provide paper or plastic bags.

We ended up camping only about six nights out of three weeks. We thought accommodations would be more expensive, but we found that the *pensionnes, zimmers, auberges,* and hotels were very reasonable if one is willing to share a bath and is not too fussy. All of the places we stayed at were immaculately clean, but some were furnished rather simply. All of the places served some kind of continental breakfast which was included in the price of the room. So that was one meal each day we didn't have to be concerned about buying.

The first night we camped, the little red Opal Ascona we had rented rolled to a stop at the entrance to a campground in Dijon, France. We had no idea what to expect. Not all of our experiences in France had been easy because so few people speak English, and with our limited French we sometimes had a difficult time.

"Could we camp here?" we managed to communicate to the proprietors of the campground.

"Oui, oui," was the answer. "Put tent on grass."

We drove into the campground and found that it was completely enclosed by a high security fence. The grass was covered with brightly colored tents of every conceivable design. Some looked like cottages with zip-up windows. Every camp trailer or caravan had a cloth room attached to the side. Everywhere people were preparing dinner, playing games, walking their dogs, or were sitting sprawled in lawn chairs.

In a few minutes we had pitched the tent, pumped up the air mattresses, and rolled out the sleeping bags. We were at home. We could not have tackled such a venture if we had not been experienced campers in our own country.

One of the campgrounds where we stayed in Switzerland was near a hot springs. A gigantic whirlpool had been installed. I jumped into that thing and thought I was going to drown—and I am a proficient swimmer. I was swept along at an ever-increasing pace through a narrow rapids and then out into a more calm area, where I was moved more slowly around to the beginning where the rapids began again. Once we got the hang of it, it was a lot of fun, and we spent hours swooshing around the pool.

We also had memorable experiences in many other kinds of accommodations. I remember a *zimmer* in Salzburg, Austria, that had starched sheets and pillowcases and an eight-inch-thick down comforter—and the temperature was about seventy-five degrees outside. Sleeping under that thing was a little warm.

I also remember Mark and Ed walking all over the fields in a beautiful valley nestled between high mountains. They could wander everywhere because there were no fences in sight. I remember hearing their voices on the patio beneath our window when they came back from their walk.

There are so many wonderful experiences to remember about that trip. I remember driving along Lake Geneva in Switzerland and passing an old castle built on a rock which jutted into the lake. A sign identified it as Chillon Castle.

Chillon, Chillon, I thought. *Why does that register something in my mind? What does it register?*

"I know something about that castle, but I don't know what I know," I told my family. "It seems like it is something about a poem I learned in elementary school. I think that's it—something about a prisoner and a castle. Let's stay near here tonight, and come back in the morning and explore," I suggested.

That's what we did, and sure enough, there is a poem called "The Prisoner of Chillon" by Lord Byron and I *had* learned a portion of it as a student.

This was a wonderful castle. We went down into the dungeon and there found the post to which the prisoner had been chained for four years. We stood in the open door wells through which the winter storms drove the lake water into the dungeon. We wandered alone and unguided for hours through halls and passageways, up winding staircases, into bedrooms, armor rooms, and into the ancient medieval hall still equipped with all of the fixtures required to feed and care for crusading knights. I think in each of our minds we stepped back in time, and we were the knights and the ladies of the court.

An Introductory Trip

This trip was meant to be an introduction to foreign travel. It was not meant to be an in-depth study of each country's culture. For that reason, we decided to cover as much territory as possible in three weeks and just sample the flavor of each of the seven countries we visited.

We began in The Netherlands where we stayed five days with friends. From there we journeyed to Belgium and again stayed with friends. After that we were on our own. We drove to Paris, and found that it was impossible to park in that city. So we drove out to Versailles and there found a lovely hotel with a small secluded courtyard and a place to park. The next morning we toured the palace and wonderful gardens of the kings of France, which are located at Versailles.

We also relocated to a hotel near the end of the subway line. This proved to be an excellent idea. It gave us quick access by train to all of Paris. I wish you could have seen us trying to figure out the automated ticket machines and the complex subway system. We finally made it by putting all of our heads together and really working at it. Learning the Parisian subway system has helped us in using the subway in many other cities of the world.

From France we crossed the Alps to Switzerland, where we spent several delightful days. Then we crossed the Alps again and headed into Italy. We went as far south as Florence, where we viewed so many wonderful works of art and cathedrals.

Then we had to make a decision about which way to return. Mark wanted to see Venice, but Wendy wanted to see Salzburg, Austria. We decided to accommodate both of their wishes. We are so glad we did, because both places turned out to be favorite stops on the trip.

After Austria we went up the Rhine River, cutting back into Brussels, Belgium, where we returned our car. Our friends from The Netherlands picked us up there and took us home with them. The next day we flew home—poorer, wiser, richer in shared experiences, and so glad we had made the trip.

Dreaming Your Own Dreams

The reason I'm telling you about our family adventure to Europe is not just to give you a travelogue, but to encourage you to dream your own dreams—and to dream them big. People ask us from time to time how we managed to make this trip. Perhaps for some families a trip to anywhere is not such a big deal, because they have enough money to do it. But for most families, struggling with braces, music lessons, education, and a host of other things, such a trip would be a major event.

No person knows what he can do until he tries to do it. The same is true for families. You don't know what your family can accomplish in terms of goals until you try.

Maybe your goal isn't Europe. Maybe it's a vacation in Hawaii, or skiing in Vermont, or taking a pack trip in Colorado, or some other exciting family adventure.

What goal would stretch your family? What goal would cause you to work together to accomplish it? What goal would set your priorities in order? What goal would give you wonderful memories for the rest of your lives?

Dream that dream. Strive toward that goal. Work together to overcome the hurdles—and achieve your dream together.

As our big jet lifted off from the same airport where we had landed three weeks earlier, I looked over at Wendy. She was crying. "I love Europe, Mom. I don't want to leave. Do you think I'll ever come back?"

I squeezed her hand and said, "Yes, I think you'll be back." Little did I know that one day God would put His hand on my daughter and say, "I want you to work for Me in Europe. Will you?"

God has big plans for your kids and your family, and He will reveal them—especially to those who are not afraid to go where He wants them to go. Conditioning our kids to be world Christians is a noble challenge. Think about it.

14

Adventure Ideas A to Z

Is your family ready to experience meaningful adventures that your children will remember throughout their lives? Here's an abundance of family adventure ideas, but don't stop with these.

Dream your own adventures—and dream them big.

Airplanes and Airports

An airport is a hubbub of activity. Go to the observation tower and watch planes come and go. Kids love it.

Watch sky divers.

Find a field from which glider planes are towed aloft.

Take the kids for a plane or helicopter ride.

Visit an airplane museum.

Antiques

Children can learn a lot about our history and will feel much closer to those who've lived before us if they can see the implements of work and leisure from earlier eras. An antique store is a good place to expose them to the past. Visit local antique shops and look for unusual items. Talk with the shop owner about those unusual items. Find out how they were used in everyday life.

Visit antique shows.

Buy one or two inexpensive items. Old postcards and photos don't cost too much.

Let the child start a collection of some inexpensive type of item—spoons, cards, matchbook covers, and so on. He'll be much more interested in going into an antique shop with you.

Arboretums

Many cities have arboretums with beautiful trees, flowers, walkways, and ponds. Usually there are playground facilities for children and picnic areas as well. Use them; they are for your enjoyment.

Take a bag of bread to feed the waterfowl.

Take a book to help you identify the kind of waterfowl you may see.

Teach your children to sit quietly observing wildlife and listening to the sound of the trees.

Play games on the lawns (if it is allowed).

Wade in the ponds.

Pick up colored leaves in the fall, and have a prize for the best one.

Take a book to help you identify the kinds of trees in the arboretum, or get a guide from the park's information system. Walk around and talk about the different kinds of trees in the park.

Archaeology

There may be archaeological digs in your areas. In many places Native American villages are being unearthed and restored. In some places original cities are being excavated. (The Seattle underground is an example.)

Visit museums that display the findings of archaeological digs.

Attend seminars and classes at museums to learn more about these digs.

Read books about the unearthing of various cultures. The saga of Masada is wonderful reading. The exploration and uncovering of the ancient city of Jericho is also fascinating.

Architecture

Architecture can be a fascinating pursuit. Most American cities have sections of wonderful old houses and buildings. Many of them have what I call "gingerbread"—brackets, turnings, rosettes, and shaped shingles.

Find a book on the architecture of your city.

Take architectural walks in your town. Check with the chamber of commerce for information about guided walks or maps.

You may want to collect interesting houses with a camera.

Look for interesting architectural details in new and restored office buildings in your town.

Learn to look up. Much of the architectural detail is above street level.

Give a prize to the one who finds the oldest building during an architectural walk.

Go to the top of some of those interesting office buildings. See if they have a restaurant, and at least have dessert there.

Art

Find out how many art galleries your city has. Set out to visit them all.

Try to get the stories behind the paintings, if at all possible.

Look for the unusual. Modern art can be very amusing.

Look for street art and sculpture. In our city we have a statue which is a group of individuals and a dog waiting for a bus. It is called *Waiting for the Interurban.* The statuary always is decorated for the appropriate season by citizens. They feel they own the statuary, and so they give the figures their coats, umbrellas, and so on.

Astronomy

Visit an observatory.

Visit a planetarium.

Buy a telescope and a chart of the stars, and start learning about them on your own.

Watch the newspaper and newscasts for unusual planetary alignments, meteor showers, comets, and other unusual heavenly phenomena.

Go someplace where it is really dark, and see how many stars you can see. It may surprise you.

Get books on stars from the library. There are wonderful, beautiful, full-color books which show close-ups of planets, nebulae, galaxies, stars, and other heavenly bodies.

Animal Shows

Animal shows are lots of fun for kids. Kids and animals just seem to go together.

Attend a cat fanciers' show.

Visit a rabbit or horse show. Talk to owners about their pets.

Attend a working-dog or a field-dog show.

The local and state fairs are animal shows. The cutest thing I've ever seen was a little girl who had fallen asleep in the hay at the state fair, just under the head of her yearling heifer. It looked as though she had been grooming the animal and had fallen asleep. Together they were lying in the straw.

Dressage and other kinds of horse shows are great fun.

Judging livestock for fairs is an interesting procedure to watch.

Many circus events have to do with animals.

Battlefields

There are hundreds, maybe even thousands, of battlefields across our country. These include the sites of Indian massacres, Civil War battlefields, American Revolutionary War battlefields, Spanish-American War battlefields, and lots of others.

Visit battlefields. Walk where history was made.

See sound and light shows often presented at battlefields.

See working dioramas which show the action of the battle.

Tour the museums usually attached to these battlefields, and in your minds try to reenact what happened there.

Learn the Gettysburg Address, which was given by President Lincoln at the Gettysburg battlefield.

Beaches

Beaches are wonderful places for families.

Walk or run in the sand.

Fly a kite.

Build a sand castle and let the waves wash it back to sea.

Collect driftwood.

Collect shells, but take them only if it is allowed.

Soak up sunshine.

Swim.

Berry Picking

Learn to identify the kinds of berries which grow in your locale. These can be either domesticated or wild. Take the whole family on a berry-picking expedition. Our family usually could pick fifty pounds of strawberries (that didn't include the ones we ate in the fields) in about forty-five minutes.

Have a berry feed, and invite all your friends to help you eat the berries.

Make jam for the whole winter, and do it as a family project. Kids like to help make jam.

Give a prize to the child who picks the most berries, or the biggest berry.

Birds

Go bird-watching.

Buy a bird identification book, and try to identify as many birds as possible.

Watch for shows of performing birds.

Boats

There are all kinds of boats and all kinds of activity that take place on the water, from canoeing to hydroplane racing. There is no limit to the kinds of adventures boats can provide.

Take a canoe trip—either for an afternoon or as part of a camping trip. Slip along the edges of a stream or lake with only the sound of the paddles dipping in and out of the water.

Take a sailboat ride with someone who knows how to sail, or maybe your family would like to pursue buying its own sailboat so the whole family can learn to sail.

Visit U.S. Navy and Coast Guard ships. Take their tours; you'll all learn a lot.

See a hydroplane race either in person or view it together on television.

Teach your kids to row a boat.

Teach them water and boating safety; it could save their lives.

Visit the tall ships when they are near you.

Ride a paddle wheeler.

Visit the U.S. Constitution in Boston Harbor.

Try to arrange a visit aboard a tugboat.

Ride a ferryboat.

Ride a hydrofoil.

Take a speedboat ride.
Learn to water-ski.
Visit research ships.
Take harbor tours and other excursion boat rides.

Botany

There are many adventure ideas that can fit under this rather bookish title. We are surrounded by plants. Our life is dependent on plants. We can have a great time together as a family discovering all that there is to know about botany.

Wild flowers: There are thousands upon thousands of wild flowers. Just when you think you've seen and identified every one in your area, you discover a new one.

Buy a wild flower identification book and see how many you can find and identify in a single summer.

Collect and press samples of all kinds of wild flowers in your area. Squeeze them in a flower press, or in the pages of a book, until they are dry. When they are dry mount them on cards and cover with clear plastic wrap to preserve them.

Look tiny. Some exquisite wild flowers are half the size of your little fingernail. Lie down in a meadow and look tiny. See what is there.

Lie in a field of daisies and watch the clouds sail past.

Take home a bouquet of wild flowers (if picking is allowed and if there are plenty of the variety of flowers you are gathering).

Make a daisy chain and wear it, or make a circlet for your hair.

Pretend you are a butterfly and flit from one flower to the next in complete abandon.

Wild Edible Plants: Buy a book and learn to identify various kinds of wild edible plants.

Make a whole meal of wild edible plants.

Conservatories: These are wonderful places, especially in the dead of winter. Visiting a conservatory is like stepping out of winter into summer.

Find out if your city has a conservatory.

When you go, try to identify as many flowers and plants as possible.

Some conservatories have live birds in them. Watch for them and identify them. They are usually very tame, and it is a good opportunity for your children to see them up close.

Mushrooms: Buy a book on mushrooms and learn to identify them. Stress to your children the importance of not eating wild mushrooms, because many can be toxic.

Take pictures of the mushrooms with a close-up lens.

See how many different kinds of mushrooms you can identify. Keep a list.

Attend a mycology exhibit.

Buy various kinds of mushrooms at your local market, and learn to cook and eat them.

Visit a mushroom farm.

Gardening: Gardening can be a family project, and one which helps to save money. Gardening can even be done in tubs on a balcony or the patio of an apartment. You don't need much space to have a little salad garden.

Work together to choose a spot for your garden.

Dig it up together.

Let the children choose the kind of seeds and plants for the garden—with guidance from you, of course.

Plant, water, and hoe the garden together. Children can learn about hard work and about responsibility by gardening.

There are many spiritual lessons to be learned from a garden. Jesus used many parables that were based on plants and gardening. Talk about these with your children.

Bridges

You wouldn't think bridges could be an adventure category, but there are so many kinds of bridges that they can be very interesting.

See how many different kinds of bridges you can identify in your area.

There are cable-suspension bridges, drawbridges, bridges that turn to let boats through, floating bridges, high-rise bridges, swinging bridges, and logs over creeks.

Visit the London Bridge in Arizona.

Walk across the Golden Gate Bridge in San Francisco.

Visit a Japanese garden and climb over the high curved bridges there.

Walk an abandoned railroad trestle for a real thrill.

Count how many bridges there are within a ten-mile radius of your house.

Find out if there are any covered bridges in your area. Visit them and take pictures. Find out who made them and why.

Bicycling

Bicycling together is a wonderful family activity. It is also good exercise. Even if there are babies in the family, they can be put in carriers on the rear wheel of Mom and Dad's bike or in a kind of trailer. I don't think I ever have seen a crying baby on a bicycle. They love it.

Find out where the bike trails are in your area. More and more trails are being developed everywhere in this country. Learn about them through the newspaper, books at your local bookshop, and regional magazines.

Spend a whole day bicycling. Take a picnic lunch to eat along the way, or plan to stop at a fun restaurant for lunch.

Go to bicycle races.

Enter your family in a bike-a-thon.

Canyons

There are all kinds of canyons to see. Some are just little narrow ones in the woods. Others, like the Grand Canyon, are too huge to comprehend.

Find out where the canyons are in your area.

What other attractions are near the canyon that might prove an adventure for your family?

Visit the massive Grand Canyon in Arizona.

Take a burro ride to the bottom of the Grand Canyon.

Visit Royal Gorge in Colorado.

Visit the canyon of the Yellowstone River in Yellowstone National Park.

Visit a canyon which has a swinging bridge hanging over it. Bounce your way back and forth across the bridge.

Cemeteries

Believe it or not, cemeteries can be lots of fun.

Find an old cemetery and go there with large sheets of white paper and black charcoal, pastels, or color crayons. Lay the paper over a tombstone and rub it with the crayon. It will bring up the pattern on the tombstone even though it may be almost unreadable otherwise.

Read the inscriptions on the tombstones.

Note the ages of those who have died. Notice that many died very young. Talk about the hardships they endured and how much better life is today.

Caves

There are four kinds of caves: limestone, ice, talus, and lava tubes. The kind most of us are familiar with is the limestone cave with stalactites and stalagmites in wonderful formations. An ice cave is formed in areas where snow recedes and leaves a huge circular tunnel. A lava tube cave is one where lava flowed out many thousands of years ago and left a hollow tube in the earth. The talus cave is formed by the laying down of debris at the base of a cliff or mountain. It is usually the result of glacial action.

Find out what caves are in your area and tour them.

Watch for caves to visit when you are traveling. There are Mammoth Cave in Kentucky, Carlsbad Caverns in New Mexico, Sea Lions Caves in Oregon, and many more in between.

Join a spelunkers' club. Spelunkers are people who explore and study caves, usually uncharted ones.

Churches and Missions

Churches and missions are fun to collect with a camera. Perhaps you have a budding photographer in your family who can learn to take good pictures of these buildings. Perhaps some day he can sell them to a publisher.

Watch for churches in the towns, villages, and cities you visit. Every town has one or two beautiful churches.

In New England watch for the white-spired churches tucked in the mountains.

In the Southwest watch for Spanish-style stucco and red-tiled-roof churches.

There are old missions all over this country. Watch for them and visit them. Many are now state parks.

Wander through the old churches and missions. Teach your children to respect these places of worship. Talk with them about the hardships early missionaries and pastors endured to bring the Gospel to this country.

View the movie *The Mission* to give them a better understanding of what it cost to open certain mission fields.

Watch for organ concerts and special events at city churches throughout the land.

Take your children to services of faiths different than your own, and help them to respect other people's beliefs, traditions, and customs.

Cities

Cities are exciting places. Pick a city—any city—and decide to visit it. Before you go, order free materials from the chamber of commerce of that city so that you know what is available to see and do there. Let your children send for these materials.

Determine to learn about that city while you are visiting there and catch the flavor of the place.

Cities have many neighborhoods, each with its own flavor. Explore these in depth. Poke in and out of shops, restaurants, markets, factories, and places of worship.

See the city's art museums, special features, zoos, parks, bridges, and downtown shopping area. Learn about its sports teams and attend a game if you can.

Clocks

Go to a clock shop and look at all the different kinds of timepieces that are available.

Watch for clocks in towers of buildings.

Watch for street clocks. There are a couple of marvelous old steam clocks in our area. It looks so strange to see steam coming from a clock.

Look for old clocks in museums and antique shops.

Buy an old clock at a thrift store. Let the kids take it apart.

Invest in a fine clock with chimes and pendulums.

Coins

Coin collecting can be a fun hobby for the entire family.

Visit a coin shop and have the owner show you his collection.

Buy some folders for pennies and let the kids start collecting.

Go to a coin show where many dealers get together and sell coins. Coin dealers are like a fraternity. They all know each other, and they soon learn about their customers as well.

Get some books to help you identify coins.

Collecting coins from foreign countries can be lots of fun and very educational as well. The study of the coinage of a certain country can create a real interest in the culture, geography, and history of that country. Collecting foreign coins is not as good an investment as collecting U.S. coins, but in most cases they cost less to collect.

If you develop an avid coin collector, invest in some gold coins for him. Some can be obtained for less than fifty dollars.

Communications

Communication facilities like TV and radio stations can provide an evening of adventure for your family.

Visit the local TV stations. Some have programming that welcomes local guests. Try to get tickets and go to the show.

Visit a radio station and watch the disc jockeys at work. It can be an eye-opening experience to your kids to see the faces of their favorite radio voices.

Get tickets to watch the filming of weekly sitcoms or other favorite network programs when you are in the Los Angeles area. Tickets are free, but must be obtained ahead of time.

Costumes

Kids love costumes, and there are all kinds of places to see them. Make an adventure out of costumes.

Go to a photo shop where they dress you up in old-fashioned costumes and have a family picture taken. It's lots of fun.

Visit a museum that has a costume display.

Go to a costume shop and buy costume-making materials.

Go to a thrift shop and buy old clothes to make into costumes.

Attend an ethnic festival where everyone is dressed in costumes.

Computers

It's definitely the age of the computer, and your kids probably know more about computers than you do. Perhaps you need to let them lead you on an adventure pursuing computers.

Visit a computer store and see what systems and games are available.

Visit a firm or factory that has a big computer operation.

Almost every home now has or soon will have a computer. Buy some new games to play together on the computer.

Cultures

Throughout this book we have talked about the interesting adventures a family can pursue related to studying the diverse cultural backgrounds of the American population. We are a divergent group of folk, and discovering that can be a great adventure for your family.

Watch for seasonal ethnic events and go to see them.

Take part in food fairs which are centered around ethnic foods.

Go to church services and celebrations that have an ethnic emphasis.

Make or buy various kinds of ethnic costumes.

Tour ethnic neighborhoods in your city.

Dams

Most dams also have a power plant nearby, and some also have fish ladders. These can be interesting to visit.

Tour a power plant.

Drive across the top of the dam, if there is a roadway and it is allowed.

Look for different kinds of dams—earth-filled, concrete, or even a beaver dam.

Look at the displays which show how the dam was built.

Find out how many dams are in your area. See how many you can visit.

Find out how the fish ladder works, and watch for migrating fish.

Deserts

Deserts look very barren at first, but they are fascinating places.
Read about life on the desert.
Rent and view a Walt Disney video that shows animal life on the desert.
Go to a desert and observe carefully.
Look for desert birds.
Look for desert animals.
Are there cactuses? What kind are they?
When do the cactuses bloom? Be there to see it.
Take a burro ride in the desert.
Enjoy the solitude of the desert.

Drama

Attend drama productions at local high schools, colleges, and theaters.
Dramatize a play for your neighbors and friends.
Watch for drama productions in shopping malls, parks, and churches.
See if you can go backstage and meet some of the performers.
Work together as a family and write a play.

Eggs

Visit a poultry farm and see how eggs are produced, candled, and crated for shipment.
Visit a hatchery and see young chicks emerging from their shells.
Eat an omelette in a restaurant that specializes in them.
Watch for a Ukrainian craftsman who decorates eggs using a wax resist-and-dye method.

Factories

Factories are exciting places to visit. There are all kinds of factories to tour. Most factories have guided tours. Take advantage of this free adventure.

       Go to a breakfast cereal factory
       See steel being made.
       Visit a fabric mill.
       Tour an automobile factory.
       Tour an airplane factory.
       Visit a food-processing plant.
       Visit a lumber mill.
       Visit a meatpacking plant.
       Tour a candy factory.

Look around your area and see what is available.

Farming

There was a time when farming was a true adventure for a family to pursue—farming was their livelihood. Now there are fewer and fewer people making their living farming, and our kids know less and less about how food is produced.

Visit a dairy barn and watch the milking process. In most large dairies, it is a high-tech operation.

Get out somewhere and see the wheat and corn harvests.

Visit a horse ranch in the spring and see the new colts and fillies.

Visit a cattle ranch at branding time.

See if you can arrange a visit to a sheep ranch either at lambing time or at sheep-shearing time.

Fairs and Expositions

Every summer there are many fairs and expositions. There's something about a fair that's unique.

Make it a day and go to the county or state fair.

Ride the rides, see the exhibits, and eat the foods.

Prepare an exhibit for a fair. Make it a family project.

Fall Color

In most areas of the country there are fall color displays. In fact, one of the national news networks gives a daily update of fall color on the morning news show.

Take a drive through a high-color area.

Learn what makes the leaves change to different colors.
Gather bouquets of leaves to take home with you.
See who can find the most beautiful leaf.
Take pictures.
Plan a vacation to New England in time to see the color.

Fashion

Attend a fashion show at a local department store.
Take a class in fashion.
Go to a local mall and see the changing fashions.
Learn how to make something to wear.
Get a book from the library and see how fashion has changed throughout history.
See what fashions have been retained over the years.
Talk and think about how fashion is influenced by well-known personalities and world events.

Feasts and Festivals

Keep checking your local newspaper for these events, and take your kids to them. There are winter carnivals, autumn leaf festivals, medieval festivals, pageants, and Native American festivals all waiting to be discovered.

Forests and Woods

There are all kinds of forests across the country. Most of them have both guided and unguided nature walks.
The forests are often on public lands and belong to all of us. We can use them free of charge.
Have a picnic in the woods.
Camp out in the woods.
Walk softly and watch for forest creatures.
Learn to know what plants and animals are in the woods. It will make the woods feel as comfortable to you as your own living room.

Forts

Old, usually reconstructed forts are interesting places to visit. They are scattered all over the country.

Visit a fort and talk about what it would have been like to live there with no running water, no sanitation facilities, no electricity, and with an enemy outside the gates.

Firefighting

Where there's smoke, there's fire; where there's fire, there's excitement. Look into firefighting in your town and area.

Visit the local fire station. Ask for a tour.

See if there is a smoke-jumper facility associated with the National Forest Service near you. Visit them and find out what they are doing.

Go see a fire, but be sure to stay out of the way.

Encourage fire safety in your children.

Talk with them about the dangers of playing with matches.

Fish

Visit a large aquarium. There are many superb ones throughout the country.

Go fishing—fly-fishing, deep-sea fishing, trolling, lake fishing, ice fishing, and fishing from a dock.

If you don't fish, go to a local fishing area and talk with the fishermen. They'll tell you all kinds of stories.

Go snorkeling, and view the fish in their own environment.

For the really adventurous, take a course in scuba diving.

Fossils

Fossils can be found everywhere. They are inside rocks, in clay banks, in gravel bars, and at the seashore.

Find out if there is a fossil deposit in your area, and see if it is all right to gather fossil samples.

Go to a museum and look at the fossil samples.

Visit Dinosaurland near Vernal, Utah, and see the unearthing of a bank full of dinosaur bones. Some scientists have worked on the same fossil for thirty years.

Furniture

Visit a furniture factory.

Visit an upholstery shop and watch furniture being restored.

Hunt for antique furniture.
Learn about different styles of furniture.

Geology

Your family can have many adventures learning about geology and rockhounding.

Visit a geological display in a museum.

Visit a mining museum.

Find out where the local rockhounds go and what they are looking for. The ideal is to get a rockhound to take you out with him.

Learn to identify the different kinds of rocks. If your kids have studied science in school, they may be able to help you.

Ghost Towns

The West has numerous abandoned ghost towns. They are fun to visit.

Try to figure out what each building's original purpose was.

Pick up bits of broken pottery and study the design.

Pretend you lived there in the town's heyday.

Glassblowing

Craft shows, fairs, and specialty malls often have glassblowers at work. Watch them.

Colonial craft exhibits sometimes have glassblowers at work.

Glaciers

If you live where there are glaciers, visit one and study what happens when a glacier moves through an area.

Look for the U-shaped valleys that indicate a glacier has gone that way in times past.

If you are visiting a glacier, look for the glacial milk which flows from beneath it. This is powder-fine silt suspended in water. It gives the rivers a milky look.

Government

Visit government buildings.

Go to see your state legislature in action.

Go to see the United States Congress in action.
Talk about government.

Hobby Shows

In most cities there are hobby shows once or twice a year. Go
to see them.
   Also in many cities there are model-train clubs.
   Find out if there is Go-Kart racing in your town.

Hot-Air Balloons

Go to the area where hot-air balloons are being flown, and
watch these beautiful creations lift off from the ground.
   Pay for a ride in a hot-air balloon for your kids.
   Talk about the scientific principles that make a hot-air balloon
fly.

Home Tours

In many places home tours are conducted to raise funds for
charities. Sometimes the homes are old, sometimes they are
large, and sometimes they are very unusual.

Insects

Collect insects and identify them.
   Get a book and learn all about insects.
   Many children are afraid of insects, but if they learn which
are harmful and which are helpful, they will lose some of their
fear.

Juggling

Learn how to juggle. Do it together as a family.
   Go see a clown who knows how to juggle.
   Watch for street jugglers.

Kite Flying

Buy a good kite and fly it together as a family. Kite flying never
loses its appeal.

Go to a kite store and see all the beautiful kites that are available.
Read about the history of kite flying.
Try building a kite together.
Watch for kite-flying exhibitions.

Lakes

Lakes offer all kinds of family fun.
Sail a boat.
Swim.
Fish.
Loaf on the shore.
Hike to high mountain lakes where only the hardy go.

Law Enforcement

Visit law enforcement agencies. See what the police department in your city does in the way of public relations.
Visit the F. B. I. in Washington, D.C.
Visit a courtroom and observe the process of law at work.

Lighthouses

Collect lighthouses with a camera. See how many different kinds you can discover.
Tour a lighthouse if possible.

Medicine

Is there an interesting medical facility nearby? Could you all learn something by visiting it? Do they offer tours?
Sometimes when a new medical facility opens, tours are available. Seeing such a facility and learning what happens there may help your children to be less afraid if they have to go to a hospital one day.

Meteorology

Visit a weather station and learn what happens there.
Keep charts and graphs of your weather.
Learn about clouds and what weather changes they signify.

Learn the dangers of lightning and thunderstorms.
Learn how hail is formed.
Look for exhibits in science museums that tell about weather.

Military

Visit a military installation.
Watch a military parade.
Learn about the different branches of the service and the uniforms they wear.

Mining

Learn about different mining operations.
See if you can tour a mine.
Some museums now have simulated mine shafts to give you a feel for the miner's lot in life.

Mountains

Take a trip to the mountains.
Go skiing.
Go camping, but not at the same time you go skiing.
Hike in the mountains.
Go to the top of the mountains on a clear day and see if you can see forever.

Music

Go to the symphony.
Go to the opera.
Go hear old-time fiddling.
Find a good banjo player and watch his fingers fly.
Listen to all kinds of music and learn to appreciate them all.
Listen to music and draw pictures about what you think the music is saying.
Write new words to an old tune.

Nature Trails

Nature trails are a good learning adventure and also a great place to run off steam.

Watch for something you've never seen before—perhaps a flower or a mushroom. You'll probably find it.

Neighborhoods

Walk through neighborhoods and learn about them.

Browse through all the little shops.

Talk to the people who live there. How long have they been there? Why have they never moved from there? What is the best feature about their neighborhood?

Oceanography

Visit the ocean beaches and walk along them while beachcombing.

Swim or wade in the ocean.

Find out where you can watch whales migrating. Some places even offer boat rides to watch the whales.

Learn about the shore birds which nest along the coasts.

Learn about life in the tide pools.

Origami

Get someone who knows this Japanese craft of folding paper into decorative objects to teach you how to do some simple pieces. Learn together as a family.

Parks

There are all kinds of parks in every city and town. Most of them have some distinctive characteristic. Find out what that is.

Visit our national parks. They are a great heritage and a great treasure. Take advantage of them.

Pottery

Pottery works are spread around the country. Some are small shops owned by individuals and some are huge factories which make dishes by the thousands.

See what's available in your area and take a tour.

Get some clay and make your own pottery.

Quilts

Hand-pieced quilts are coming back in fashion. They are sold at top dollar as true works of art.

Visit a quilt show and see some modern craftsmanship.

Visit a museum where old quilts are displayed. Remember that these were made without the aid of sewing machines and modern conveniences. All work was done by hand.

Rodeos

Rodeos are wild, fun events. Take your kids and enjoy the performance of cowboys and animals.

Talk to a cowboy or cowgirl.

Skiing

More and more families are learning to cross-country or down-hill ski. Cross-country skiing probably provides more time for family togetherness than downhill, but most young people prefer the speed of downhill skiing.

Once you learn to ski, there are all kinds of places to go skiing.

Snowmobiling

Snowmobiling is an increasingly popular sport. Many families belong to snowmobiling clubs and get out regularly in the wintertime.

Sports Events

There is no limit to the sports events your family can attend at any season of the year. Professional sports are expensive, but there are many local sporting programs that are virtually free.

Learn a sport and play it together.

Theme Parks

There are a number of great theme parks around the nation, such as Disneyland, Walt Disney World, Seaworld, and Six Flags Over Texas. They are great fun for families.

Toys

Toy stores are fun for the whole family to visit. Even if you don't buy a lot of toys, it is still fun to look and maybe even try out the display models.

Transportation

Learn about all methods of transportation. Remember that as your children become familiar with all modes of transportation, they will be unafraid later in life to travel on their own and continue to have their own adventures.

Take a boat ride.
Take a train ride even if it is just to the next city.
Visit a switching yard for trains.
Ride in a double-decker bus if possible.
Take a bus trip.

Universities and Colleges

If you hope that your children will attend college, then it is a good idea to introduce them to some of the campuses in your area.

Attend a play on the college campus.
Attend a musical event.
Visit the campus museum.
Go to the college library.
Have lunch in the student union building.
Look at some of the colleges' catalogs, especially if your children are teenagers.

Vegetables

Visit a farmers' market and try some new fruits and vegetables you've never eaten. Let the kids make the selections.

Talk to the farmers. Learn where they grow their vegetables, why they grow them, how long they've been vegetable gardeners, and anything else you can get them to tell you.

Grow a vegetable garden.

Waterfalls

Visit as many in your area as you can find.
Photograph waterfalls.

Wood Carving

There are still some fine craftsmen who do wood carving. Find them and watch them at work.

There are shows which display driftwood which has been polished to a furniture-like finish.

Xylophones and Other Musical Instruments

Go to a musical instrument store and talk to the owner about the various kinds of instruments he sells.

Visit someone who makes musical instruments.

Invite someone who plays a musical instrument to your home, and have him share his music and something about the instrument (the more exotic the better).

Have the children make their own musical instruments from combs and paper, pot lids, empty cardboard boxes, and other household items.

Make your own xylophone by filling glasses with water to various levels.

Yacht Racing

If you are in an area of the country where they are held, attend a yacht race.

Watch the America's Cup yacht races on television.

Try to find someone with a yacht and have him take you for a ride.

Zoos

Who doesn't love a zoo? Kids do, that's for sure. You can go again and again, and each time see something you never have seen before.

Help your children learn to be observant and quiet when watching the animals.

15

The Adventure Continues

"Mom, I had a really exciting adventure," Wendy told me on the phone recently. "I had to go to The Netherlands to pick up some people who were coming to work on the new church. Usually it takes about two hours to drive up there and two hours to come back. But the fog was so terrible that there were accidents everywhere. There were seventy cars off the road in various places. I sat without moving for more than an hour near Rotterdam."

"Don't tell me. I don't want to know about it," I told her. "I don't like to hear about you in dangerous circumstances."

"Ah, Mom, don't worry. God's taking care of me," she told me.

We'd come a long way since I'd looked for the instruction book pinned to her diaper. We'd taught her to value an independent life-style, to be unafraid of new adventures, and to be willing to serve God wherever He called her to be—and she was doing it.

I don't worry much. I know worrying is useless, and I know He is watching out for her.

A couple of years ago Ed planned a ministry trip to Southeast Asia with some contemporaries. He asked Mark if he would like to go along on the trip. Of course, he wanted to go. The only problem was that he would have to part with all the money he had saved since he was four years old.

"Do you think I should do it, Mom?" he asked. "It's a lot of money, and it has taken me a long time to save it."

"Go Mark! Buy yourself an experience no one can take away from you."

"But maybe I should get a new car."

"You could, but you may never have the opportunity to take this kind of a trip with your dad ever again. You make up your own mind."

A few months later a brand new 747 airplane carried Ed and Mark off on a five-week adventure to Hong Kong, China, Malaysia, Singapore, and the Philippines. Mark had learned well to value experiences over things.

Ed's and my adventure in parenting is about finished. It has been an exciting adventure. Through it, not only the kids, but also Ed and I have learned to treasure people, ideas, and shared experiences. We have learned to grasp the moment and enjoy it to the fullest because there is no guarantee that a particular moment—a special experience—ever will be repeated. It probably will not.

This book is for all those who yet have the adventure ahead of them or are in the middle of raising kids. It's offered with the prayer that your adventure in raising your kids will be even richer, fuller, happier, and more exciting than ours was. And may the God who gave our children to us and who watches with great interest over our families guide you and keep you as you "talk . . . when you sit in your house and when you walk by the way and when you lie down and when you rise up" (Deuteronomy 6:7 NAS).